ELDERS' TRAINING

OTHER CRUCIAL MATTERS CONCERNING
# THE PRACTICE OF
# THE LORD'S RECOVERY

BOOK 4

WITNESS LEE

*Living Stream Ministry*
Anaheim, California

First Edition, December 1985.

Library of Congress Catalog
Card Number: 85-82043

ISBN 0-87083-195-X (hardcover)
ISBN 0-87083-196-8 (softcover)

Published by

*Living Stream Ministry*
2431 W. La Palma Ave., Anaheim, CA 92801 U.S.A.
P. O. Box 2121, Anaheim, CA 92814 U.S.A.

*Printed in the United States of America*
98  99  00  01  02  03  /  9  8  7  6  5  4  3  2

# CONTENTS

# FOREWORD

During February of 1984 over three hundred and fifty brothers from six continents gathered in Anaheim, California with Brother Witness Lee for a two week international elders' training. The messages that were released at that time are the contents of this four volume set. Book one presents the essential aspects of the ministry of the New Testament; book two sets forth the vision of the Lord's recovery; book three covers the way to carry out the vision; and book four emphasizes other crucial matters concerning the practice of the Lord's recovery.

Those of us that were in these meetings were deeply convicted of our need to be further enlightened by the Lord concerning God's economy and concerning the intrinsic essence of the New Testament ministry which is for the carrying out of this divine economy. As the Lord's recovery is continually spreading throughout the world, these messages are more than crucial and urgently needed. We believe that they will render a great help in preserving all the saints in the central lane of God's economy, without any deviation, for the fulfillment of His eternal plan. Our hope and expectation is that these messages will become a governing and controlling vision for all in the Lord's recovery. May we prayerfully consider all the points presented in these books and accept them without any preferences.

November, 1985                                        Benson Phillips
Irving, Texas

# Chapter One

# CONCERNING THE USE OF
# REFERENCE BOOKS AND OTHER WRITINGS

## (1)

I believe we have seen in a sufficient way that we need to help the saints to get into the full knowledge of the truth. In this chapter I want to begin to fellowship concerning the use of the reference books and other writings.

### CHURCH HISTORY AND CHRISTIAN WRITINGS

The church has been existing on this earth for over nineteen hundred years. Even from the first century, immediately after the time of the apostles, writings began to come out. Luke 1:1 indicates that there were more than four who wrote an account of the Savior's earthly life. There were also many epistles written besides what we have in the New Testament today. Eventually, however, only four of the gospels written by the earlier saints were chosen to be in the Bible and only a certain number of epistles were chosen out of many epistles. This shows us that even the writings in the first and second century were not all quite accurate for the study or the knowing of the truth. This also helps us to realize that we cannot follow the so-called Christian writings without any discernment.

The so-called church fathers also wrote many things after the passing away of the early apostles. The writings of the church fathers have become a big field in much of today's theology. The church fathers' writings plus the councils with their creeds turned the church into Catholicism, and the papal system was fully established by the end of the sixth century. The papal system stopped the councils and the creeds because from that time onward whatever the pope said was the final word.

This kind of situation issued in what historians call the Dark Ages, which lasted about one thousand years. During this time the Bible was locked up and was not allowed to be read by the laymen. This period of the Dark Ages compelled some of the Lord's faithful ones to reconsider the situation. This was the beginning of the Reformation, which actually started before the time of Martin Luther. None of the reformers actually intended to leave the Catholic church. Their intention was just to correct, to adjust, and to bring back at least some basic truths. History tells us, though, that Luther and most of the reformers had to leave the Catholic church, and according to the political situation of that time most of them went along with the formation of the state churches.

Since the Reformation, many books were published which are all considered as Protestant writings. This also opened the door to give the freedom to all Christian writers. Whatever they liked and felt burdened about, they were free to write. More books came out by the state churches and by the private churches such as the Baptists, the Brethren, the Presbyterians, the Moravian Brothers, and then the Methodists. Throughout church history a great many books were written. Nearly no other field in human culture has so many thousands of different publications as in the field of Christianity.

## CHRISTIAN THEOLOGY

As we have pointed out, the so-called theology in today's Christianity is not just of one school. Christian theology has a least four or more major schools. Catholic theology is one major school, and it may be called sacramental theology. Then there is reformed theology, mostly based upon the teachings of John Calvin. This kind of theology also had much to do with the Reformation, which was under the leadership of Martin Luther. Then later on we can see dispensational theology, which is the theology of the Brethren. The Brethren are very much for Calvin in the matter of predestination, but they would not go along completely with reformed theology.

Then there is what I call secular theology. This is not taught in the theological seminaries or Bible institutes, but in the secular universities which have schools of divinity. Their teaching of theology is what I would consider as a secular item. Even some theological schools are not so pure for theology itself, but are more in the realm of studying the Bible as a type of literature. We may call this kind of theology academic theology. All the books which are published and on today's bookshelves come out finder these main schools of theology. Today in the United States we see all these kinds of theologies with their students.

Even among the Christian publications today the situation is quite confusing. It is hard to say which theological school is fundamental. Some claim to be fundamental and they use the term "orthodox doctrine," but to some the orthodox doctrines are only those teachings which Jesus taught the twelve disciples directly while He was on this earth. If this were the case, however, then more than half of the New Testament books would be cut off. Fourteen of the twenty-seven books of the New Testament were written by Paul, who was not one among the twelve while the Lord Jesus was on this earth in the three and a half years of His earthly ministry. This kind of thought about orthodox doctrine is completely wrong. A few years ago at a certain conference, a number of Christians held up a banner which said, "We don't follow Paul, we follow Christ." Also, a number of years ago there was a conference held in Chicago which called people to go back to the early councils of the church before the papal system was established.

## TWO RISKS

If we help the believers in the Lord's recovery by using these books, we run two risks. First, we unintentionally bring the Lord's recovery back to the old books which the Lord's recovery has gone through already. From Brother Nee through our sixty year history, we have gone through those books. I do not mean that starting from Brother Nee we have read through all the books. This is impossible. However, mainly through Brother Nee's work of looking through thousands of spiritual books and expositions, the Lord's recovery has gone through all those old writings. Brother Nee also had much fellowship with me concerning the things he researched, and I learned much. I really appreciate Brother Nee. In my whole Christian life, I have never met one who had his degree of spiritual discernment. He was the top selector. Among the many books he looked into, he was able to make a quick selection of the books which were useful. This is why I say the Lord's recovery has gone through all those old writings as a collective unit. Although I did not study in a Bible institute or a theological school, I am able to give you an analysis of the so-called theology in today's Christianity. Many of these old writings are very good, but some of them are not good and are misleading, distracting, holding back, and some even destroy the faith.

Second, we run the risk of bringing the recovery backward and not onward. Since we began to go through these books, the Lord began to show us something further. History tells us that the Lord's recovery did not begin from Luther. Actually the Lord's recovery began from the fourteenth century. Since that time, the Lord's recovery of the truth has been continuing all the time. It did not stop at Luther and it has not stopped with anyone. The problem is, though, that the followers of certain faithful brothers received the light, yet they all stopped with what they received. The followers of Luther stopped at the Lutheran faith, and the followers of John Wesley stopped at the Methodist faith. Even the followers of the Brethren stopped with Darby, but the Lord would not stop and He was never stopped. He kept going on and on. Brother Nee told me during his time that in both Europe arid America the Lord had no way to go on. The Lord was forced to go to China, "a heathen land." Brother Nee considered that in that time as far as the Lord's recovery was concerned China was a piece of "virgin soil." He told me the Lord was forced to come to virgin soil to carry on His recovery. I have no doubt about this because when I was with Brother Nee I did see something new. What I had seen was not something new in the Bible, but something new in discovery and something new in recovery of the already existing items in the Bible. Even within the past twenty-two years in the United States there have been quite a number of crucial recoveries and discoveries of the biblical truths. The Lord's recovery is something going on. It is not something going back.

The meeting hall in Anaheim was designed to have a big library downstairs. I intended to fill this library with all the classical books from the church fathers' writings down to the present time. I also intended to have three or more readers, who would read all these books on certain major subjects such as the Triune God. They would read these books, make notes on them, and if needed even xerox certain paragraphs from them. Then whenever we write something for publication, we would not need to spend much time going to the books themselves. All we would have to do would be to go to our notebook. This would save us a lot of time in our writing. Then the news went out that there was a kind of trend. The saints thought we were going back to the old doctrines and some even came to me and said, "This is good because this shows people that this is not only Witness Lee's writing, but all the writings of Christianity are here." When I heard this, I immediately made a decision to stop what we had intended to do. I had even bought a set of writings in Latin on microfiche which was quite expensive, and we had built a table for reading this microfiche, but after I made this decision we returned it. The reason why I stopped what we had intended to do was because I saw the peril that this would bring the recovery back. We would not be going onward but going backward. Gradually, however, we collected the needed reference books, and whatever was needed we collected.

## THE NEED OF A BASIC KNOWLEDGE
## OF THE BIBLICAL TRUTHS

I also strongly indicated that we should charge our young people to learn the biblical languages of Hebrew and Greek. If possible, they should also learn the theological language of Latin. I did this because I fully realize that for the long run the Lord's recovery needs the basic knowledge of the biblical truths. To acquire such a basic knowledge in a full and complete way, our young people need to learn Hebrew to study the Old Testament, Greek to study the New Testament, and Latin to study the earlier theological writings. My encouragement to study these languages was somewhat misunderstood. Also, some others thought that I wanted them to go back to the old books, so they began to collect them.

Two young people came to me who were quite stirred up to study these old books. They asked me to give them a list of all the reference books and expositions for them to study. I immediately told them that I would not give them such a list. I advised them to do their best firstly to learn Greek and if possible Hebrew. I did not include Latin because Latin is not that important. I also told them that if they mean business with the Lord and His truth they must spend five years to study all the publications the Lord's recovery has ever put out. I told them that they had to spend two hours every day to finish this course of the Life-study Messages with the Recovery Version, including the footnotes and the cross references. Finally, I advised them to come to me after they had finished their course and then I would give them a good list of reference books. I said this because at that time they will have been educated and built up with a strong footing of the truth. Then they will have the best discernment. They will be able to look into books and immediately discern whether they are a help or a hindrance.

Actually, we must realize that in the older theological writings, we may be able to find different terminologies and expressions, but there is no new item there concerning the truth. In the past sixty years, by His mercy, we have picked up all the basic items of the divine and spiritual matters. After you have received a good foundation in the basic truths of the divine revelation, you will be fully established. You can then go back to see the things in the older books. The positive items in these books would strengthen and confirm what you have already seen and will enrich your speaking so that you can show people what is right. Then you would never be misled.

## THE RISK OF GOING BACK TO THE OLD THINGS

If we go back to the old things without proper consideration, we run the risk of opening the door for all the saints to go back to the old things. If we are not the Lord's recovery, we need to get into the old things. Otherwise, we have nothing. Today's seminaries train their people to study all the old publications. They study church history, the historical study of theology, and the writings of the church fathers. They have degrees in theology, Hebrew, Greek, church history, and other items. The seminaries give people doctor's degrees, but these degrees are in the old things. What they are actually doing is holding the Lord back. Today's theological teachings hold the Lord back from going on in His recovery. I am not saying that all the books in the past are not good. Some of them may be good, but they are old. Some of you who graduated from a seminary can testify that you did not receive anything advanced or improved there. All you received were the old things.

## THE NEED OF PROPER DISCERNMENT

To read others' old books needs quite an amount of proper discernment. Since I came to the United States, in my speaking I have rarely referred you to some other writings. I did this purposely. Books such as Andrew Murray's *The Spirit of Christ,* however, I did have and still have the peace to refer you to. When I was writing the notes for the book of Luke, I asked my helpers to turn to Dean Alford for a certain point. I used Dean Alford very much, but his interpretation of this certain point was absolutely wrong. This shows that we must have the proper discernment in reading the others' theological writings.

The first year of my study of the Bible and of the so-called theological matters was in the year 1925. The books I first received were mainly from reformed theology. I was very much interested and burdened to know the seven parables in Matthew 13. I collected the books which the reformed theologians had translated into Chinese. Their theological teaching told me that the leaven referred to in Matthew 13:33 was very good. They say it is the influence of Christianity, the influence of the biblical truth, or the entrance of the gospel. Eventually this gospel will influence the entire world and the world will become a utopia. They also say that the big tree in

Matthew 13:31-32 was something positive. I was wondering about their teaching.

A year later, I began to contact the Brethren. They taught me exactly the opposite. At the beginning I was wondering who was right. The books I had read by the reformed theologians were translated by the missionaries in China and were published by the top Christian publication firm in Shanghai. The local Brethren Assembly I was attending, however, was small. An old British brother taught there all the time. I had to consider and weigh which teachings to take.

## TAKING CARE OF THE YOUNG ONES

I passed through this stage of picking up wrong interpretations and concepts of the Scriptures, so I learned something. I do not like to see that the Lord's recovery is being brought backward to the old writings. I also do not like to see that the young generation would be brought back to the old things to occupy them. We must realize that we only have one life to live. Even with two or three lives, you cannot exhaust the reading of the Christian books. I do not like to see people misdirected in reading things that will waste their time.

By the Lord's mercy, there has been a kind of laboratory work done through Brother Nee and us. We have picked up the necessary, basic items of the divine, spiritual, and heavenly things. We have put all these things, not in a scholarly form, but in a "layman's form" which is John's form in the book of John.

My burden is that we must take good care of the young ones among us. Do not bring them into peril so that they would be occupied with the wrong things. We have a pure system of publications which comprise all the main things of the divine, spiritual, and heavenly things. These publications are very adequate for all the young saints among us to have a good foundation laid and a strong standing established. Then they could go on, not to learn more things from the old books, but to check the old books and to get themselves confirmed.

For us to bring the young ones into the old books without consideration is a peril and a risk. It is not safe. What you young ones can use as reference books, however, are the dictionaries, lexicons, and concordances. Nearly all the dictionaries have some good points. No dictionary, however, is complete and all differ from one another. Never be satisfied with one. You must use more than one. When you investigate a word, do not be satisfied with one dictionary's definition. You must look into others. These are the only things which I would recommend for you young ones to use—the lexicons, the dictionaries of languages, and the concordances of the Bible. You should use these references in the way of comparison. This will help you.

## THE BASIC PRINCIPLE OF INTERPRETATION

This does not mean that we are exclusive or narrow. This means, though, that you will not be spoiled or damaged. I must repeat again that to understand the types you must be taught with certain principles and then you are safeguarded. To interpret the prophecies you must know the basic principles of interpretation and then you are safeguarded. To interpret any verse of the Bible you must keep the basic principle taken by all the sound Bible teachers. The unique, basic principle is that to interpret any verse you need the entire Bible. Firstly you need the context of that verse, then you need the context of the entire book, and finally you need a bird's-eye view of the entire Bible. Then you are safe in interpreting any verse.

To say this, however, is easy. The ones who declare that the Father in Isaiah 9:6 is the Father of eternity and not the Father in the Godhead may also say the same thing. They may say that to interpret the Bible you need to take care of the context of the verse, the context of the book, and the context of the entire Bible. Actually, however, when they interpret Isaiah 9:6, they do not take care of this principle.

In interpreting or explaining any portion, even any verse, of the Bible, if we do it without keeping this basic principle, we will not be safeguarded from making mistakes, even terrible errors. I would like to spend a little more time to show you how I take care of this basic principle in my further study, thus far, of Isaiah 9:6 as follows:

Since this verse is written in the Hebrew poetic way of expression, and Hebrew poetry goes often in pairs, the first two clauses, "unto us a child is born, unto us a son is given," form one pair. By just saying a child, we do not know whether this child is male or female. The second part, a son is given, defines the gender of the child. Born and given are also a pair. This indicates that to be born is to be given. There is, though, a small amount of difference here. You cannot say that to be born is just to be given or to be given is just to be born. There is a difference that needs to be taken care of. In like manner, a son is different from a child. The expression "a son" gives you more denotation than a child. A son may be a child, but a child may not be a son. A child is born, but a son is given, which matches John 3:16 saying that God has given us His only begotten Son.

The son in this verse bears two main denotations. One is that the son is the son of a human virgin who was born of her (Isa. 7:14; Matt. 1:23). The other denotation is that the son is also the Son of the Most High. Gabriel told Mary in Luke 1:32 that the One conceived in her womb would be called the Son of the Most High. In this sense the son was not to be born but to be given. This being given, though, is related to being born. The son as the son of Mary with the human nature was born, and the son as the Son of the Most High with the divine nature was given through the son of Mary's being born. This wonderful Son was not only born of the human source, but also given from the divine source. He is both human and divine. This is the very God-promised Messiah to Israel (John 1:41, 45), who is Jehovah Himself to become, by being born of a human virgin (Isa. 7:14), a man by the name Jesus—Jehovah the Savior (Matt. 1:21-23) to be the Christ in God's New Testament economy (Matt. 1:16). As such a one, His name is called: "Wonderful, Counselor, The mighty God, Father of eternity, The prince of Peace." According to the composition, "Wonderful Counselor" [King James Version puts a comma after Wonderful, which should be deleted] and "mighty God" should be one pair, and "Father of eternity" and "Prince of peace" should be another pair. This Wonderful Messiah, as the child born to the children of Israel and a son given to them, is a Counselor, even a Wonderful Counselor to them, who gives them the wonderful counsels all the time and does everything for them. To them He is also God, even the mighty God, who is able to carry out whatever counsel He makes for them as their Counselor. In addition, He is also their Father, from eternity as their source, who fosters them and takes care of them all the time from eternity and through all the generations. He is also a Prince to them, who is their peace, gives them peace, and brings them into peace.

"Father of eternity" does not indicate eternity's Father, but the eternal Father, just like "Prince of peace" does not indicate peace's Prince, but the peaceful Prince. The Messiah, who is the Wonderful Counselor and the mighty God to His people, Israel, is not eternity's Father, but His people's eternal Father. According to the context of Isaiah 9:6, whatever Messiah is is His people's. He is His people's Wonderful Counselor, His people's mighty God, His people's peaceful Prince, and His people's eternal Father, not eternity's Father. This corresponds with the context of the entire book of Isaiah in 63:16 and 64:8. To say that "Father of eternity" is in the sense of eternity's Father, or indicates that He is the originator of all creation, does not fit the context either of the verse of Isaiah 9:6 or of the entire book of Isaiah. This kind of interpretation is like a foreign article wedged into a living body. Whatever is mentioned in Isaiah 9:6 is related to Israel, the people of Messiah, not to any creation. The Father of eternity in this verse must be the Son to be the eternal Father of His people.

I hope this shows you that it is not so easy to interpret the Bible, especially a verse like Isaiah 9:6. Do not go to the old books in a light way and believe whatever you pick up from the old books merely by your present capacity of discernment.

### THE NEED OF FURTHER DISCOVERIES AND FURTHER VISIONS

God's holy Word is rich and profound. We need further discoveries and further visions in seeking the truths contained in the holy Scriptures. I would like to share with you one of my further discoveries as follows.

When Brother Nee asked me to stay for a few months in Shanghai to begin the work with him, I did. While I was staying there, Brother Nee did a number of things to put me on the test to find out where I was, what I was, and how much I could do. One of the tests involved a special gospel meeting which the church in Shanghai made a decision to have. I was happy about this decision because I wanted to hear Brother Nee's preaching of the gospel. At that time, I was staying above the meeting hall, and on the evening of the gospel meeting I was looking forward to listening to his preaching. About less than half an hour before dinner time, a brother knocked on my door and handed me a note from Brother Nee. The note said, "Witness, please give the message tonight for the gospel preaching." I had no thought or idea that I was going to be asked to speak, and the meeting would be shortly after dinner. Brother Nee did not let me know that he wanted me to preach until the last minute. I had no idea what the Lord wanted me to speak. Eventually, a burden rose up within me to preach on John 16:8-11. These verses tell us that when the Spirit comes, "He will convict the world concerning sin, and concerning righteousness, and concerning judgment; concerning sin, because they do not believe in Me; and concerning righteousness, because I go to the Father and you no longer behold Me; and concerning judgment, because the ruler of this world has been judged." WhWhen this burden came to me I was happy and I was strengthened. I became bold.

I told the people that evening that sin is related to Adam (Rom. 5:12). We were born of sin in Adam and as long as we remain in Adam we are sinful. Righteousness is related to the resurrected Christ. In verse 10 the Lord says that the Spirit convicts the world concerning righteousness because He goes to the Father. This points to His resurrection and ascension and indicates that redemption has fully been accomplished. Therefore, if we believe in Him, He is righteousness to us (1 Cor. 1:30), and we are justified in Him (Rom. 3:24; 4:25). If we believe in Him, we will be transferred out of Adam under the sinful condition into Christ on a righteous standing. The Spirit convicting the world concerning judgment refers to Satan. Satan has been judged and will be eternally judged. If we do not repent of the sin in Adam and believe in Christ, the Son of God, we will remain in sin and share the judgment of Satan for eternity (Matt. 25:41). Therefore, sin, righteousness, and judgment actually refer to three persons—Adam, Christ, and Satan. These are the main points of the gospel. The Spirit convicts the world with these points. We were born into Adam, and we have to believe into Christ to be transferred out of Adam and into Christ. If we do not, we will have a part with Satan in bearing his eternal judgment.

When I stood up to speak and looked around I noticed that Brother Nee was not there. Quite a time later he and I were taking a walk together. He told me that while I was preaching that evening on John 16, he was standing outside a door close to where I was standing. Only a door separated him from me. He told me that he had been listening to my message. He also told me that in China not many Christian teachers knew the Bible in this way, and he encouraged me to go on to bear the burden to preach and to teach the truth. It was really a further discovery and a further vision to me that in John 16 sin, righteousness, and judgment refer to Adam, Christ, and Satan. This took place in 1934.

# CONCERNING THE USE OF REFERENCE BOOKS AND OTHER WRITINGS

## (2)

### ACQUIRING A PROPER FOUNDATION

We have seen that we should not bring in any distractions or frustrations to the Lord's ministry. I do not mean that we do not have the liberty to read the old books. We should not exercise any control over the saints. This is absolutely wrong. Please do not think that in my fellowship concerning the way to use the reference books and other writings I intended to control the saints from reading others' writings. This is absolutely wrong. You are free to go to any books, but if you go to the books I would say you run a risk, and you will probably waste your time. If you ask for my advice, I would say that you had better not go to others' books until you have finished the course of the Life-study Messages and the Recovery Version with the footnotes to get a strong footing and a proper foundation which gives you the best discernment. Then it is safe for you to go into other books.

### SPIRITUAL BOOKS

I would also like to give an illustration of having the proper discernment in reading the spiritual books. *Pilgrim's Progress,* which was written by John Bunyan, an Anabaptist, was one of the top selling books next to the Bible. It was even more popular than George Cutting's *Safety, Certainty, and Enjoyment,* which is a booklet concerning the assurance of salvation. Despite the popularity of *Pilgrim's Progress,* if you look into this book with some discernment, you can see that there is very little stress on Christ as life. The main theme of the book is that Christians need a full separation from worldliness. *Pilgrim's Progress* helps one to get out of the world. When I was in the Southern Baptist elementary school in China, *Pilgrim's Progress*, translated into Chinese, was a textbook in the classes. Many Christians received the help from that book to be separated from the world, but they could scarcely see any stress on Christ as life in it.

## SPIRITUAL BIOGRAPHIES

I also would like to fellowship with you concerning the reading of spiritual biographies. The better Christian biographies are those concerning people like Hudson Taylor, George Müller, D. L. Moody, and Charles Spurgeon. All these biographies are profitable in a number of points concerning the individual Christian life. They are very helpful to some extent, and I personally have received much from these biographies. I read most of them in my youth. We must realize, however, that the Lord's recovery has brought us absolutely back to His New Testament economy and the New Testament ministry. We must also realize that the twenty centuries of church history are a history of the deviation from these two points—the New Testament economy and the New Testament ministry. Actually, not one of the spiritual biographies is cleansed from the matter of division.

I appreciate Hudson Taylor's life greatly. I received much help from his life. We must realize, though, that even with him the element of division was still there. There was nothing wrong with him picking up a burden to bring the gospel, the Lord's name, and the Bible to China. This was altogether God's doing and I do believe that the burden which came to him was from God. I appreciated that from my youth. I am not speaking this in a light way, because we have paid very much attention to the China Inland Mission which was founded by this dear brother. We always considered that this was the top mission to China and was very scriptural, spiritual, and evangelical. After we had seen God's New Testament economy with

God's New Testament ministry, however, we could not absolutely say amen to this mission.

This does not mean, however, that we were as strong as John Nelson Darby was concerning Hudson Taylor. In the late 1800's the Lord raised up Hudson Taylor with a burden to bring the gospel to China. This was during the same time when the Brethren Assemblies were very prevailing. John Nelson Darby and George Müller were living at this time. These two brothers were the top brothers among the Brethren. They eventually held different opinions concerning the matter of receiving the believers. Darby felt that since denominations were condemned by Paul as something of the flesh and thus something sinful (1 Cor. 1:10-17; Gal. 5:20), anyone who joined a denomination or remained in a denomination was a "companion of sin." He felt that the Brethren Assemblies could not receive a "companion of sin." To join the Brethren Assembly, you must leave the denominations absolutely and officially. They used to ask people to write a letter to their denomination asking them to take their name off the membership roll. It had to be very official. This was the reason why Darby was condemned as being very exclusive, and we cannot agree with him in this point.

George Müller did not agree with this either. He said that you should not consider a brother such as Hudson Taylor a "companion of sin." Hudson Taylor was George Müller's friend in the Lord, and George Müller greatly helped the China Inland Mission financially. George Müller maintained that Hudson Taylor's personal Christian life might have been better than some of the brothers in the Brethren Assembly. As a result of these differing opinions, there was a division among the Brethren. This was the origin of the so-called Exclusive Brethren and the so-called Open Brethren; the leader of the Exclusive Brethren was John Nelson Darby and the leader of the Open Brethren was George Müller.

On the one hand, I agree with George Müller and not with John Nelson Darby. He was wrong in this point. Hudson Taylor was called by God and received his burden for China from God. This was wonderful. In China I never said anything or did anything to discredit the China Inland Mission because I appreciated their work of bringing the gospel to the interior of China. That was a marvelous work which I appreciate and treasure. On the other hand, we cannot deny that even with this wonderful work there was an element of deviation which still remained.

This element of deviation can be seen in the practice of the China Inland Mission concerning the matter of the church. The China Inland Mission collected many devoted believers to pick up the burden to go to the interior of China to preach the gospel of Jesus there, yet all these believers came from different denominations. Some were Episcopalian, Methodists, Baptists, Presbyterians, and some even came from the Brethren. Hudson Taylor was very general. The decision was made that if you joined the China Inland Mission to bring the gospel to the interior of China, you could establish a church according to the denomination you came from. If you came from the Methodists, you could establish the church in the interior of China according to the Methodists. If you came from the Presbyterians, you could establish a Presbyterian style church in the interior of China. Therefore, under the name of China Inland Mission, the divisive forms of denominations still remained.

China Inland missionaries under the leadership of Hudson Taylor tried not to bring divisions to China, but they compromised with all the divisions. Actually, in the eyes of the Chinese Christians, the China Inland Mission was the same as the other denominations. Some of the denominational forms were still there under the one name of the China Inland Mission.

I agree that Hudson Taylor's biography is a great help to the individual Christian life. However, once a reader gets the help from that book, it might be hard for him to have a clear and accurate view concerning the church. Mostly, the reader who receives so much help from such a book would just "swallow up" the whole book. Even if the reader did not swallow the entire book, there would be an unconscious entrance into his being concerning this deviation. Some young saints who read this book might think, "Could such a great evangelist who was used by God to such an extent be wrong? Could he be wrong in the way he established churches?" Then there would be a question in this young one's mind concerning the recovery. This shows us that the subtle serpent is here. I passed through this stage as a young man. When I read Hudson Taylor's biography I unconsciously asked myself whether or not he could be wrong. I asked myself whether or not we could be right in this matter. By the Lord's mercy, I had passed through many kinds of testing situations before I read his biography. Thus, I was not affected.

We must consider the young ones among us. In such a biography some germs are there. The food is nourishing, but are you sure that the germs there would not poison the eater? This biography is very good, but it is not absolutely pure. At least, some element of deviation is there. Truthfully speaking, we must also realize that Mrs. Howard Taylor, who was Hudson Taylor's daughter-in-law, was a good writer who was very promoting. This is why I stopped the publication of my writing of Brother Nee's biography. I am still considering whether or not I might be promoting there. I do not like to give people an impression that I am writing a biography of Brother Nee just to promote something. One must be a very pure person to write a biography or a history without promoting.

### CONDUCTING THE SAINTS TO THE RIGHT WAY

We do not need to control the saints, and even more we do not need to stop them from reading what they want. As leaders in the Lord's recovery, however, we should conduct the saints to the right way. We do not need to tell them not to go a certain way, but we must tell them to take the right way. We are here for the Lord's recovery. The publications which can help and serve the Lord's recovery in carrying out His New Testament economy for the fulfillment of His heart's desire, I still would say, are the Life-studies, and the Recovery Version with the notes. Since this is the case, why would we not wisely conduct the church toward this way? For example, if someone asks us the best way to drive to Phoenix, we should conduct him to the straightest way.

We are not here merely for the individual Christian life, a

mission work to the foreign field, or bearing the Lord's name to the heathen countries. These are all good things, but this is not our commission. Our commission is to let the Lord carry out His New Testament economy by His New Testament ministry. This is why I feel very sorry that in certain places the leadership was not that strong or adequate. If the leadership in that part of the world had been strong and adequate, it would have conducted all the saints in every church to the right way. We should not waste time, we should not delay people, and we should not let confusions come in. We should not fail the Lord in His New Testament economy.

CHAPTER THREE

# THE REGION OF THE WORK

# (1)

## THE CHURCH BEING LOCAL
## AND THE WORK BEING REGIONAL

In this chapter we will consider the region of the work and the relationships between the regions and the churches. There is a need of a clear view of the region of the work among us in the Lord's recovery. In *The Normal Christian Church Life* Brother Nee said something about the region of the work. One sentence from this book should be quite impressive to all of you—Brother Nee said the church is local and the work is regional. Every church is local. It cannot be extra-local. The work, however, is regional and not local.

## TWO REGIONS NOT TWO WORKS

Brother Nee said this based upon the fact that the Bible reveals that the work of the Lord on this earth as the New Testament ministry had two regions. The first region was in Judea, which was mainly among the Jews, and the second region was in the Gentile world, which was mainly for the Gentile churches. It is also clear that in the record of the New Testament, the work in the region of Judea for the Jewish churches was under the leadership of Peter, and the work in the Gentile world for the Gentile churches was under the leadership of Paul (Gal. 2:7-8). This is also clearly recorded in the book of Acts (Acts 1:15; 2:14; 9:15; 22:21).

Some would take a standing to say that these were two works—one for the Jews in the Jewish land and one for the Gentiles in the Gentile world. One work was by a group of

workers having Peter as the leader, and one work was by a
group of workers having Paul as the leader. We must realize,
however, that the Lord does not have two moves on this
earth. He has only one move. Also, the Lord does not have two
bodies on this earth. He has only one Body.

## ONE MOVE, ONE BODY, AND ONE TESTIMONY

Actually, in this one Body there is no difference between
the Jew and the Gentile. Every kind of distinction has altogether disappeared in the Body. In the Body there are no
regions and there are no Jews or Greeks. For such a Body the
Lord only has one work on this earth. From the New Testament we can see that the Lord has one move on this earth,
one Body, and only one testimony. According to space and
time, His New Testament move, His Body, and His testimony
are universal. These three aspects must impress us very
deeply. The Lord only has one move, one Body, and one testimony.

While the ministry is going on, it is regional. This does not
mean, however, that the Lord has different moves in different
regions and that He has different bodies and different testimonies. This does not mean that the ministry or the work
under Peter's leadership in the Jewish land was for one kind
of testimony, and then the work and the ministry under the
leadership of Paul in the Gentile world was for another kind
of testimony. The Lord has, in the New Testament age, one
unique ministry for one move to produce one unique Body as
one unique testimony.

## THE EXAMPLE OF THE DECISION IN ACTS 15

Based upon this, we can see that the Judaizers, the Judaizing believers, tried to overcome the Gentile believers at
Paul's time. They tried to convert the Gentile believers to be
Jewish. They attempted this strongly and this caused trouble. The regional work under Peter's leadership was recorded
in the first twelve chapters of Acts. From chapter thirteen of
Acts, the record of the Lord's New Testament ministry turned
to Paul. This means that the ministry turned to the Gentile
world from Antioch. Then Paul and his co-workers went out

to the Gentile world to preach the gospel and to set up the churches. The Lord moved to establish His Body in the Gentile world to bear a testimony in the typical, heathen, pagan world. After chapters thirteen and fourteen of Acts, trouble came in chapter fifteen. This trouble came, not from the Gentile region, but from the Jewish region. It came not from the ministry under Paul's leadership, but from the ministry under Peter's leadership, which was much under the influence of James. Chapter fifteen of Acts tells us that the Judaizing believers came down to Antioch, which was the very origin of the ministry to the Gentile world, and they brought the problem there (v. 1). That became a real damage to the Lord's ministry, His Body, and also His testimony.

Paul could not tolerate the situation. Under that situation, he could not go on with the Lord's ministry to continue the Lord's testimony among the heathen. Therefore, he and Barnabas went up to Jerusalem to have some fellowship to solve the problem. The decision made at the conference at Jerusalem should not be satisfactory to the readers and teachers of the Bible, who know God's New Testament economy. The concluding word given by James was still under the influence of the Mosaic law, due to his heavy Judaic background. The influence of this background still remained, even at the time Paul paid his last visit to Jerusalem (21:20-26). One point, however, was established in Jerusalem. This point is that the Lord's testimony is one, the Lord's Body is one, the Lord's ministry is one, and the Lord's move is one. If the Lord's move, the Lord's ministry, the Lord's Body, and the Lord's testimony had not been one, Paul would not have needed to go to Jerusalem, and there would have been no need for them to make a decision which covered not only the Jewish believers but also the Gentile believers.

The decision in Acts 15 was not made merely by the Jewish region or merely by the Gentile region. Actually, it was a decision made above the regions and beyond the regions. The decision made covered all the churches, whether Jewish or Gentile. This does not mean that the churches in Judea can keep the law and the churches in the Gentile world do not need to keep the law. This also does not mean that the

churches in Judea bear one kind of testimony and the
churches in the Gentile world bear another testimony. It is
not like the United States where every state has its own laws.
According to the basic principle of the New Testament economy, the decision made in Acts 15 is not so satisfactory to us.
However, no one can deny that a principle was established
which covered all the churches. The American constitution
allows every state to have its own laws, but this decision
made at Jerusalem did not allow the churches in different
regions to have their own law, which means to have their own
testimony. We must see this.

**LOCAL ADMINISTRATION
YET ONE BODY
BEARING ONE TESTIMONY**

In the United States, the Californians can say that they do
not need to keep the laws in New York or Texas, and the
people in Illinois can say that they would not keep the laws in
California. According to the decision made at the conference
in Jerusalem, however, a principle was established that all
the churches should keep the same kind of "law" and bear the
same kind of testimony. Whether Jewish or Gentile, all the
churches are just one Body and all the churches bear one testimony. In their administration the churches might be
different from one another in their locality, yet their testimony should still be one because they all are one Body under
the one ministry and one move of the Lord. This is my burden
in this chapter. I hope this could be impressed into you.

The reason why I am sharing this at this time is because
in the Lord's recovery over the entire earth, there are signs
coming out to indicate that there is a certain realization that
the churches in different regions under certain kinds of work
have the freedom to be different. For instance, the brothers in
the Far East may think that the testimony there and the
Lord's move there should be different from the United States.
They could take a strong excuse that they are not Americans,
but that they are Chinese. They also may feel that they can
be different because they were at the initial stage of the
Lord's recovery and the United States came into the Lord's

recovery later. On the other hand, some of the American saints may think that they are Americans and that they could not be the same as the oriental brothers and sisters in the Lord's move for His testimony. You may have never heard such a word or have said such a word, but such a thing is secretly hidden there and has crept in unconsciously. This is an illustration between the continents, between the eastern hemisphere and the western hemisphere. Also, the African churches may feel that they can never be the same as the American churches, and the South American churches may think that they cannot be the same as the European churches.

The United States is quite large with fifty states and with over eighty churches in the Lord's recovery. I think many of you have an impression and the tendency to think that the work is divided into regions and that certain regions would not touch other regions. Also, these regions would not be touched by other regions. No one has said this, but the situation already exists in this way. It seems as if every region has its own jurisdiction just like a local church has its own jurisdiction. We must realize that every church should have its own local jurisdiction, but this is only for administration. It is not for the testimony or for the Lord's move.

## An Example of Local Administration

Let me give an example to illustrate what I mean by the legislation or jurisdiction being for administration. The number of meetings which the church in Anaheim should have cannot be decided by the church in New York. Neither can it be decided by the church in Cypress. Although Cypress is so close to Anaheim, this should and can only be decided by the church in Anaheim.

## Examples of Items Related to the Body

Some may ask whether or not the receiving of a brother is a local administration matter or something related to the Body. We must realize that to receive a brother is very serious. Receiving the saints is quite crucial because this decides whether or not you are sectarian. If your receiving of the saints does not cover all the genuine saints, that receiving is sectarian. By this we can see that the receiving of the saints is not merely a local administration matter because it affects the Body of Christ. If you receive every genuine believer, you are a part of the Body representing the Body and not a sect representing yourselves. However, if you receive the saints according to your taste, this is sectarian. We should not say that receiving the saints is merely a local matter.

A decision to have seven meetings a week or four meetings a week is merely, purely, and singly a local administration matter. This does not affect any other local churches and has nothing to do with the testimony or with the Body. To receive the saints on the positive side and to exclude the saints on the negative side, however, means a lot because it affects the entire Body. You should not consider this as a local matter because this is a matter belonging to the Body. If you exclude one from your local church, you exclude one from the Body. If you are not receiving one into your local church, you are not receiving one into the Body. This aspect is above the regions and also above the churches. It is a Body matter and not just a local church matter.

Let me cite another illustration to show that something done by a local church may not merely be a local church matter, but fully related to the entire Body. For a local church to receive a ministry that is different from the general ministry which produces the churches, establishes the churches, and is still edifying the churches affects the entire Body. Paul's ministry was a general ministry to produce the Gentile churches, to establish them, to edify them, and to help them grow. I refer to Paul's ministry as a general ministry. Then Apollos came in with another ministry. For the church in Corinth to receive such a ministry, they must consider the effect of receiving such a ministry. Undoubtedly, you have the right to receive any ministry because you are a local church. However, you must consider that your receiving of such a ministry is not merely a local matter. This is not like making a decision as to how many meetings a local church should have.

We must also realize that for a local church to print and distribute publications affects the testimony of all the churches. When a local church puts out a printed testimony it should be done in a very careful way with much consideration as to how this would affect the Lord's testimony universally. We must always consider the effect of what we do on all the local churches.

These three illustrations are good enough and strong enough to tell us that it is not right to think that just because we have a regional work with a few churches under this regional work, we have the full jurisdiction to do everything according to our choice without caring for the Lord's universal testimony, universal Body, universal ministry, and universal move. If we think and practice in this way, we will get in trouble, and we will make trouble for others. Every local church does have its own jurisdiction, but whatever a local church does must be done in a careful consideration as to how this would affect the Lord's universal testimony, universal Body, universal move, and universal ministry.

## An Example from Our History

I would like to give an illustration of what I mean by relating a situation among us in the past. There was a certain local church which I loved and did my best to help and to keep it on the right way. The Lord knows and some of the other brothers know how much I did my best to keep that church from going astray. Some information came to me about this particular locality which said that this locality thought they had the best way to practice the church life. They claimed that the church in Los Angeles was just the training center and that it did not have the proper practice of the church life. This kind of fellowship went to Atlanta and that bothered the brothers there. Therefore, the brothers passed on the information to me.

One day the leading brother of this locality, who thought they had the best way to practice the church life, came to see me. I told him that if he felt that their way was the right way to practice the church life, I would not say anything. I also told him, though, that I did not think it was wise for him to go out and particularly to go to Atlanta and tell the saints there that Los Angeles is only good for a training center and does not have the proper church life. I told him that it was not wise to tell other churches and other saints that the best way to practice the church was in their locality. I also told him that this would damage him and cause trouble to the churches.

To some extent this brother promised not to do this anymore. Then, I myself went to visit there purposely to see whether what I heard was true or not. When I was there, they told me that they were going to have the Lord's table early in the morning because they wanted to take care of the infants. When I went to attend their Lord's table, I saw that they even fed the infants with the bread. When I saw that, I had the full realization that this was off. However, I did not criticize and I did not tell anybody. I kept this in my heart, thinking that as long as they practiced this way by themselves it would be all right. I did not want to adjust them, and I did not want to bother them.

A good number of the saints from this locality came for the summer and winter trainings. After they had attended the trainings, they were troubled when they went back to their locality. On the one hand, they were in their locality for a half a year under that certain kind of practice. When they came to attend the training for ten days, however, they tasted the general flavor in the Lord's recovery. Because of this they did not feel so good about the particular situation when they went back. Then there was an attempt in their locality to limit the number of the saints who could come to the trainings. This caused a lot of trouble and the trouble reached a certain degree where the leading brother in this locality could not tolerate it any longer. As a result, two brothers were excommunicated.

When I heard this, I had nothing to say. These two brothers then came to me and told me that they did not consider what was in their locality as a church in the Lord's recovery. Actually, it was not, but it was a sectarian thing. Then these brothers asked me what they should do. I asked them what they felt, and they said they felt that they should begin to meet as a church in the recovery and not as something sectarian. I told them that if they felt this way they had no choice but to be faithful to their feeling according to the Lord's leading. When they began to meet, to their surprise about one-half of the saints there immediately came to stand with them.

Who can be blamed for this division? The brother who took the lead in that locality should blame himself. His practices actually were sectarian because they were hard for the Body to swallow. The Body could not take it. It is not just that the ministry could not stand it. The ministry stood up with it as much as it could. I did not say a word, but eventually the Body could not swallow it.

The brother in that locality may have thought that this was absolutely a local matter and that the church there had a local administration. I admit that there was a local administration there, but what happened there affected the Body and affected the testimony. A number of saints would not agree with feeding the Lord's table to infants of one or two years of age. I hope this gives us a further realization not to think that the church in our locality has the full jurisdiction to do whatever it feels is right. You have the right to do it, but you must consider the result, the issue, and the effect.

### REGARDING THE ONE BODY— TAKING CARE OF THE LORD'S TESTIMONY

Remember that you are not the only local church on this earth. The distance between the churches means nothing, especially due to the fact that we are living in an age of modern means of communication. Any church on the earth can be reached in a matter of seconds by means of a telephone call. Whatever you do in your locality is a part of the Lord's recovery. We must take care of the churches, the Body. We must ask ourselves, "Could the Body take this? Could the Body say Amen to us?"

In practice there were regions during Paul's and Peter's time. However, we must realize that it would have been wrong for the brothers in Judea to say that they were in one region and that Paul who was with the Gentile churches in another region should not bother them. It is wrong to have the attitude that the churches in another region have nothing to do with us. Whether we are in Jerusalem, Rome, Corinth, or Antioch, all the churches are one Body bearing one testimony.

Some of you may feel that through my fellowship I am now trying to carry out Catholicism and that this is the "Catholic Church." Actually, the word "catholic" is a good word, but it has been spoiled, damaged, contaminated, corrupted, and ruined by the so-called Roman Catholic Church. All the churches should be catholic. We should be under one catholic move, bearing one catholic testimony. We should be this way because this is one Body. We should not consider that just because we brothers are working in a certain region covering a few states that this is our region. Thank the Lord that you began the work there. Peter also began the work in Judea, but if he thought that was his region and not Paul's region, that would be wrong. Thank the Lord that He used you to begin the work in that state or in those two states. Thank the Lord that He used me to begin the work in California. However, if I consider that California is my region and not your region this is wrong. We cannot do this.

I believe that Peter never thought this way and Paul never had this concept. When Paul encountered the problem from the Judaizers, he immediately went to Jerusalem. He did not say, "Forget about Jerusalem. That is not my region and the brothers from that region should not come here any more. If they come, we will shut them out and exclude them. They are the Judaizers." This is not the way Paul took. He rather went to Jerusalem. He did not tell Peter to come to Antioch to solve the problem since Jerusalem was the source of the trouble. It seems that he had the right to do this, but instead he went to Jerusalem humbly. He went neither to fight nor to argue.

The record in Acts 15 shows us the sweet spirit of the Apostle Paul during the conference held there. Mostly he did not say much. After Peter said something, Paul testified to the dear saints in Jerusalem, telling them what the Lord had been doing through his ministry (vv. 7-12). Then James said something to conclude the conference (vv. 13-21). Actually, I do not believe that the conclusion was satisfactory to Paul.

Paul, however, took this decision. This is a good example for us to follow because Paul regarded the fact that the Lord had only one Body. Whatever they were doing there was only under one move to carry out one ministry to produce the one Body that bears one unique testimony.

I do not care what kind of burden you pick up to do in your locality. I am not concerned with whether what you are doing is right or wrong. My concern is that your kind of doing might be divisive. You may have the right to do things, but the Body would not swallow them. Rather, the Body would either spit out or vomit what you do. Then you will suffer. This is quite serious. We must realize that we are not doing a piece of Christian work. We are burdened to carry out the Lord's recovery for His unique Body to bear His unique testimony.

Whatever you do, please consider the situation in this way. What you do might be better than all the others' doings. Even so, you must consider how this would affect the Body. Would this be taken by the Body? We are not a political party nor are we anything earthly. We have no arms and we do not need to fight, but the Spirit of the Lord in His Body means a lot. Do not forget the example which I related to you in this chapter. The fruit was swallowed by the doers. We must regard the Body, honor the Body, and take care of the Lord's unique testimony.

## ONE MOVE THROUGH ONE MINISTRY
## TO PRODUCE ONE BODY
## TO BEAR ONE TESTIMONY

I must testify that I really treasure the Lord's one move through the one ministry to produce the one Body of Christ to bear the one testimony of Jesus, which is of God's New Testament economy. The more I consider this point, the more I feel that this is marvelous and excellent that we could have such a reality on the earth today.

Today's world has become so small. It is nearly like one big city in the ancient times. In the ancient times, if you lived in a big city, you might not have heard the news of what happened in your city two or three days before. Today, however, whatever happens all over the earth is made known to us within even less than a few hours by telephone, television, and radio. We can fly all over the earth in a matter of hours.

Because the earth today is so small, this is the golden time for the Lord's lovers to bear His one testimony, the testimony of the one Body of Christ. Here on this earth people can see such a testimony among people of all nationalities and races over the entire globe. Wherever you go, these people speak the same thing, minister the same thing, do the same thing, and bear the same testimony. If you go to Japan, Hong Kong, London, India, Israel, or Africa, you can see the same testimony.

Just to keep such a wonderful testimony is more important than anything. Even if I were a great Bible teacher and could teach the Bible to throngs of people, this work is not as worthwhile as keeping such a testimony. Even if I could do a great evangelical work and bring hundreds of people to the Lord, this is not as worthwhile as keeping such a testimony. I hope our eyes could be opened to thoroughly see what is more valuable. If our vision is so clear, we will be rescued from being distracted by any smaller points. To center on how to meet or on any kind of work is altogether not as worthwhile as keeping such a testimony. I do believe that the Lord's blessing is really here. Many of us can testify that when we touch things other than this testimony, the anointing is not with us that much. However, whenever we touch this testimony, we experience a living, rich anointing and there is a "jumping" within us. This is a strong proof that what the Lord wants today is such a testimony. He has been seeking such a testimony for two thousand years, and this is the real revelation that the New Testament bears and conveys to us.

We must stress again and again that God's New Testament economy by His New Testament ministry is wonderful. I do not want to convince you, but I want to present such a vision to you. You compare. Here is a big diamond and a wristwatch for you to chose from. Would you rather have the diamond or the wristwatch? A wristwatch is not bad, but it cannot be compared to a diamond. Why are we so foolish to treasure the wristwatch and neglect the diamond?

I am so thankful to the Lord that He caught me in 1932. I

cannot deny that I saw something from that year onward. I would never regret that I took this way and have been taking this way for over half a century. I am so glad. As a brother among you I want to tell you that my heart is for nothing except this one testimony. I do not care for position, I do not care for rank, and I do not care for anything; my heart is only for this one testimony. I have labored and worked for this. When I was in the small town of Chefoo in China, I labored for this one testimony. When I was in the biggest city in all of China, Shanghai, I labored in the same way. When I went to Taiwan, which was a rather "primitive island" when we were there thirty-five years ago, I labored for this one testimony. I labored and labored and labored, and the Lord blessed it. Then I came to the United States, which is the top country on this earth. I labored in the same way for the one Body of Christ to bear the one testimony of Jesus. Why have I labored all these years? I was caught by a vision. I cannot deny this. Many times my wife and children, because they loved me and cared for my health, tried to slow me down. However, they knew that they could not hold me back, and they became subdued. Instead, they helped me in the Lord's work. This is wonderful!

What a mercy that we could be in such a testimony around this globe with different races and with all nationalities. If some of your friends or relatives would visit from five to ten churches around this globe and behold such a testimony, they would turn this way. They would be shocked by such a testimony. They would say, "We have never seen such a thing. In Singapore, Hong Kong, Manila, Taipei, Tokyo, Los Angeles, Dallas, Cleveland, and New York we saw the same thing. What is this?" This is the unique testimony of Jesus. In the United States, which is the top country of the so-called Christianity, strictly speaking, there has never been such a testimony of Jesus. The Christian testimony today is division, confusions, different kinds of teachings, debates, fightings, and denominations. This is what the worldly people see concerning Christianity. If we would be faithful to the Lord throughout the fifty states of the United States, wherever

people would go to visit us they would see the same thing—
the unique testimony of Jesus. This is wonderful!

# CHAPTER FOUR

# THE REGION OF THE WORK

## (2)

### THE LOCAL CHURCH AND THE BODY, THE UNIVERSAL CHURCH

The Epistle to the Ephesians was not written in a clear way to tell us exactly to which church this book was addressed. This has been a debatable subject in church history. "In Ephesus" (v. 1) is not found in earlier manuscripts. There is a question as to when the words "in Ephesus" were inserted into the manuscript. Some good Greek manuscripts indicate that this Epistle was not definitely written to Ephesus. In other words, it was not written definitely to a particular local church.

In this entire book of six chapters the only definite reference to the local aspect of the church is in 2:22. The building in verse 21 is universal and the building in verse 22 is local. The word "also" in verse 22 indicates these two aspects. Undoubtedly, this book was written to a certain locality, but the general concept of the book is concerning the Body of Christ, the fullness of the One who fills all in all. Chapter two of Ephesians is actually concerning God's universal dwelling place.

Concerning the practice of the church life, we must stress the local church. Without the local church, you could not have a practical church life. However, concerning the testimony that the church bears, we must stress the Body, which is the universal aspect of the church. These two aspects are definitely and distinctly revealed in Romans. The first eight chapters of Romans cover two main items—justification and sanctification. These items are mainly concerning the individual believers. Everyone must be justified and sanctified. The second half of Romans is also of eight chapters. Chapters nine through twelve are on the Body and chapters thirteen through sixteen end with the local churches. Concerning the testimony of the church, we must stress the Body. Concerning the practicality of the church, we must stress the local church. Without the local church, the Body would be something in the air. It would not be practical. With the testimony of the church, however, we must be extra-local and the Body must be stressed.

Sometimes expositors might be forced to say that a church in a locality is a local Body. This may be said temporarily. Actually, not one local church is the Body. Every local church is a part of the Body. The Body can never be divided into localities, but in the sense of the churches, they are in different localities. There are many local churches but there are never many bodies. We must see this and we must be balanced.

The tragedy is this: when Christians should pay attention to the local churches they take Ephesians as a refuge, saying that the church is universal; when they should take care of the universal testimony, they "run away" from Ephesians and take Revelation 1:11 as a refuge, saying that every local church has its own jurisdiction. The seven epistles to the seven churches in Revelation 2 and 3 are all different from one another. The seven lampstands, however, are absolutely not different. They are altogether the same in nature, in shape, in makeup, and in function. Today when Christians talk about the church, they should cover the local churches, but they run away from Revelation and go to Ephesians, taking Ephesians as a refuge. When they should bear the testimony of the one Body, they run away to Revelation and give up Ephesians. In Revelation 2 and 3 every local church is different, but in chapter one the seven lampstands are not different in any aspect. They are absolutely the same in size, in quality, in standing, in shape, in makeup, and in function.

## ONE MOVE THROUGH ONE MINISTRY
## TO PRODUCE AND BUILD ONE BODY
## FOR ONE TESTIMONY

The ministry of the New Testament was carried out first by Peter's company. Then the New Testament economy was carried out further by Paul's company. Peter's company was mainly for producing the churches among the Jews in the Jewish land, and Paul's company was mainly to produce the churches among the Gentiles in the Gentile world. In the New Testament, however, the revelation is more than clear that these two regions with the Jewish and Gentile churches were one move by the Lord through one ministry to produce and build one Body for one testimony.

Based upon the New Testament, we must see that on this earth today the Lord has only one move by one ministry. This ministry is not your ministry, my ministry, nor anyone else's ministry, but the ministry of the New Testament. This is why we began this training by seeing what the New Testament ministry is. The New Testament ministry is the unique ministry, and by His mercy the Lord has shown it to us.

### THE PROBLEM OF REGIONAL FLAVORS

Now we must see a basic problem that we are facing and even that we may be in. Due to certain environments and certain political situations on this earth the Lord's move, although by one ministry, is in different regions. This fact may influence us to think that each region should be different from other regions, that each region should have different churches. We may think that in Europe they should have European churches, in Asia they should have Asian churches, in Latin America they should have Latin churches, and in the United States they should have American churches. I think that this is not only unconsciously existing in our mentality, but it also might be expressed in our practice.

Even in the United States some part of the nation began to have the churches through a certain worker. Then another part of the nation began to have the local churches through another worker, and a third part of the same nation began to have churches through another worker. Due to the different workers, naturally, automatically, and spontaneously there are different regions of the work to carry out the Lord's recovery in different churches. We must see that a hidden problem is here in the different regions. No co-worker has ever said anything about this matter, but unconsciously, unintentionally, and even subconsciously, a very solid and deep difference exists in the real situation.

Let me use one region as an illustration of what I mean. This certain region always bears a special flavor. Among these brothers in this region there is an unconscious, unintentional, and subconscious feeling that their region and all the churches in their region bear the same flavor. Although the brothers in this region have never said this, such a thing does exist. There is not only such a feeling among these brothers, but also to some extent this is their practice. When these brothers are talking together and another brother from another region comes up to join them, they immediately stop talking and change their subject. The subject which they were talking about is over because a "foreigner" from a "foreign region" has come to join them.

I am happy to say though, that another particular region does not bear any flavor in a good sense. The brothers who go out from this certain region do not bear their regional flavor. Some brothers from other regions bear their regional flavor wherever they go.

The principle of what I illustrated to you applies to the whole recovery. We are all in the recovery, but mostly we bear a regional flavor. This is not scriptural because all the members in the Body of Christ, whether Jew or Gentile, should bear the same flavor. As long as we bear different flavors, this secretly and unconsciously is killing the unique and genuine testimony of Jesus which is being borne by the Body.

## THE LAMPSTAND

In Revelation 1 there are seven different localities—Ephesus, Smyrna, Pergamos, Thyatira, Sardis, Philadelphia, and Laodicea. In these localities are seven different churches, but their signs, the lampstands, are absolutely identical. When the seven lampstands are put

together, it is impossible to distinguish between them unless
you number them. When they are put together, they lose
their identity because they are exactly the same. An "Ephe-
sian type" or any "local type" of lampstand cannot be seen.
All the lampstands are of the same type, the same appear-
ance, and the same kind of shining. All the lampstands in
Revelation 1 bear the same one testimony of Jesus (v. 9).

## Snuffing Out the Differences

Although the Lord Jesus pointed out all of the differences between the seven churches, He pointed out these
differences in a negative and rebuking way. Actually, all
the differences were brought in against the one testimony of
Jesus. In Revelation 1 the Lord Jesus appears as a High
Priest trimming the lamps of the lampstand. In typology in
the book of Exodus we are told that in the morning and in the
evening the priest had to dress the lamps (Exo. 30:7-8) which
involved doing two things: first, to snuff the burned out wicks
and second, to add oil to the lamps. To dress the lamp is to
trim it by snuffing the burned out wicks and then by filling
the lamp with oil. In every epistle to the churches in Revelation 2 and 3 the Lord is snuffing the burned out wicks. In
every epistle the snuffing scissors are there. On the one hand,
the Lord was filling the lamps with the Spirit. The Spirit
speaking to the churches is the oil. On the other hand, the
Lord Jesus was snuffing the charred wicks of the lampstands.
In these two chapters the Lord Jesus as the High Priest is
dressing the lamps by snuffing the burned out wicks and by
filling the lamps with the speaking Spirit.

We must realize that there are differences among the
churches. These differences, however, do not justify us but
condemn us. The Lord has no intention of keeping or preserving these differences. Rather, He wants to snuff them out. For
example, Thyatira was the only church in which there was
Jezebel. Jezebel, however, is an extremely negative item
(2:20). This negative item in the church in Thyatira was the
biggest difference among the seven churches which the Lord
had to destroy. In Revelation 1 the standard is that all of the
churches must be the same in God's nature, in Christ's shape,

and in the Spirit's expression. In the gold, in the shape, and in the seven lamps, all the churches should be exactly the same, yet actually they are not. The churches picked up many things from their localities which became differences that the Lord needed to judge and deal with. This is the proper way to interpret Revelation 1 through 3.

This is why I told you before not to go to the books which are not trustworthy. Some books would point out the differences of the seven churches as their strong base to say that we should not try to unify the churches or to make all the churches the same. They feel that every church has the freedom to preach and to teach whatever they feel is right. Actually, though, if our practice is this way, a lot of Jezebels will be brought in instead of being destroyed by the Lord. This kind of teaching encourages the black differences, but the Lord would judge and deal with all the black elements.

We have no ground to use the differences of the seven churches in Revelation 2 and 3 in a positive way. There is no justification for these differences. Rather, they are all condemned. Some expositions, however, take these differences in a positive sense to encourage the local churches to be different from one another. The churches are encouraged even purposely to make themselves different. These expositions say that a local church should purposely go a different way in order to show that it is a genuine, typical local church with its own jurisdiction. We must realize, though, that this is altogether from the self. This is an interpretation with no heavenly vision and is altogether natural and from the natural mentality. These expositors forget that the seven lampstands as the signs of the seven churches, are pure and golden in the same shape with the same nature for the same function.

## The Testimony of Jesus

We all must see that regardless of how many regions and how many workers there are, the Lord's testimony must be one because there are not two Lords or three Lords, but only one Lord moving on this earth. Therefore, there is only one move by one ministry to produce one Body to bear the one testimony. We must consider the real situation among us. Regionally, some of the churches bear different flavors. The churches should not bear the flavor of their region and should not give people the impression that these are churches of a certain region. The impression the churches should give people is a genuine, unique testimony of Jesus. There should be no nature, no flavor, no color, and no shape of any region. The churches should only be a testimony of Jesus.

## BEING TESTED CONCERNING
## THE PURITY OF OUR HEART

We are here for the Lord's recovery, and we love Him and His recovery. We all have been tested, though, as to how pure our love is for Him and how pure our heart is for His recovery. Standing before the Lord and before all of you brothers, I want to give my testimony that I always check with myself in this way—"how pure is your heart toward His recovery? How pure is your heart toward this ministry? Are you pure in this ministry or are you using this ministry for some subsidiary purpose?"

Undoubtedly, we are using this ministry for the Lord's recovery. Everybody sees this, but could we say that our heart is so pure to such an extent that we do not have any subsidiary purpose? Quite often I check myself until I can say, "Lord, by Your mercy and for Your love I am here. If I am not pure, Lord, purify me. Purify my heart and purify my motives. Lord, I am in fear and trembling of having some subsidiary intention in Your ministry." We all have to be tested, brothers. I am not here preaching any doctrine, rebuking anyone, or justifying anyone. As an old, yet little brother I am fellowshipping with you in my honesty. I called this urgent training with a strong purpose because I realized that the purity was doubtful and questionable. We all must see that we are here for the Lord's recovery, and the Lord's recovery is just of the Lord's one move by the Lord's one ministry to produce His unique Body for His unique testimony.

## The Work of the Lord

If we try to justify ourselves by what we do, this means nothing. Are we on this earth doing different works in different regions and bearing different colors with different flavors? If we do this and we say we are for the Lord's recovery, then what kind of recovery is this? Honestly speaking, I want to tell you that no work is ours. The work in California is not mine, the work in Texas does not belong to the Texan brothers, and the work in the Northwest does not belong to the brothers there. The work is the unique work of the Lord (1 Cor. 15:58; 16:10).

## The Church of God, the Church of Christ, and the Church of the Saints

All the churches raised up by the work are not our churches. In the New Testament there is only the church of God (1 Cor. 1:2; 10:32), the church of Christ (Rom. 16:16), and the church of the saints (1 Cor. 14:33; 1 Thes. 1:1). There is not a church of the apostles in the New Testament. The apostles are the slaves serving the churches. Paul says in 2 Corinthians 4:5, "For we do not preach ourselves, but Christ Jesus as Lord, and ourselves as your slaves for Jesus' sake." I have a question mark, though, about some of you. You are trying to build up yourselves, and you do not consider yourselves as slaves to the churches. No church belongs to any apostle or to any worker. This is the missionary way. All the missionaries who went to China claimed that what they raised up was their church. If they were sent by the Baptist Mission, they raised up a Baptist Church. If they were sent by the Presbyterian Mission, they raised up a Presbyterian Church. We must ask ourselves whether we also claim our churches. Of course, we all would say that we never claimed the churches in this way, but we must consider what is unconsciously there in our heart.

I do believe that even the angels could testify for me that I never considered any church as my church. Some people accuse me of controlling, and some have even said that I control the Far East with a "remote papal system." One brother from one of the churches in Taiwan recently testified that the leading elder in his locality was altogether against my ministry for six years. This brother also testified that during these six years I did not do anything. For six years this leading elder was against me to the uttermost. He brought in a kind of pentecostal teaching and publicly told people in the meetings that he found contradicting portions in my Life-study Messages. I never did anything, however, to vindicate myself or the ministry. This is just one example which shows that I do not control the churches. All of us must reconsider where we actually are. There are many subconscious and subtle things hidden within us.

## Ambition and Pride

All the problems are due to two old "gophers"—ambition and pride. If our ambition plus our pride had been killed, there would never be any problem. We like a position. We like to be honored and highly regarded by people. We may not say this, but we must be honest before the Lord. What has been within our heart? If we were not ambitious, we could never have trouble with others. If we do not have ambition and if we do not have any element of pride, we would have no problem with anyone. When I heard about that case in Taiwan, it did not bother me.

Could you stand this kind of test? Think about the real situation around you. Why do you need to be afraid that you would be cut off? Because of the subtle thing hidden within you—ambition. You want to keep your position. If you are not afraid of being nothing, you would never think that people would cut you off. To try to preserve your position and to safeguard it is the foolish way to keep your position. This does not work.

In the church position is just like a dove. If you do not want it, it comes to you. If you want it, it flies away. When I first came to San Francisco, I saw some doves on the street. When I approached them, they flew away. When I walked away, they all flew back to the same spot. Position is like a dove. If you want it, it flies away. If you are hunting for position and you want to have a position, you will never get it. If you say that you do not want position and if you flee from it, it will come to you. To keep a position, the wisest way is not to have it. If you want to grasp a position, the position is gone already. It is not yours because you are not qualified to keep that position.

This is something very subtle which has killed all the Christians during the past centuries. Why have there been power struggles among many Christians and Christian groups? The reason is the ambition for position. I hate to see that this kind of element would come into the Lord's recovery. We all must admit, however, that we are still human. On the one hand, we are saints. On the other hand, we are still human. I must testify that day after day I was trembling before the Lord. I prayed in such a way: "Lord, thank You for another day to live You. I need Your mercy and I need Your preserving grace. Without this, Lord, You know I am still natural. I am still so much in my self in the old creation. Lord, You know that immediately without Your mercy and grace, I would live according to my flesh. I need You, Lord." If we have a heart which is not so purified but rather mixed up with a main purpose for the Lord's recovery and a subsidiary purpose hidden for ourselves, whatever we do will cause us trouble.

## The Need to Be Clean and Pure

While I was still living in Taiwan, my daughter needed to be operated on. An American brother in Taipei, who was our family doctor, told us he needed a clean place where he could perform the operation. He told us that a certain room was not qualified to be used for the operation, because while he would be operating some germs might come down from the ceiling. I was also told that in surgery all the knives and instruments in the operation must be fully clean and sterile with absolutely no germs. If there are any germs, the operation can bring these germs into the patient. This experience helped me very much. A great many times I told the Lord, "Lord, I must be clean. If I am not clean, then when I touch Your work my unclean hands would bring germs into the saints."

I began to learn this one lesson in 1932. During that year, I realized that a certain sister needed a good Bible. I had the intention to buy her one and to give it to her as a gift. Immediately within me I was checked. The question came to me,

"Are you purely of the Spirit?" I dared not to answer. This did not mean that I had any sinful or dirty intentions. I did not do anything for a few days until I was fully checked by the Lord. Then I could say that I was fully pure to give this Bible to the sister without letting her know who gave it to her. This was the beginning for me to learn the lesson that all my motives should be purified to touch the work of the Lord, to touch the church. Otherwise, I would unconsciously bring germs into the church, into the saints, and into the Lord's work. In this chapter, I am preaching the gospel you need. You need to hear this gospel. Even during this training I have checked with myself, "You are going to hold this training with all the leading ones. Are you pure? Can you say that you are so pure that you would never bring any germs into the brothers?" I am always in fear and trembling before the Lord to allow Him to purify my intention and my motive.

## The Need of a Clear Vision

In order to have this kind of dealing, we need a clear vision of the Lord's move, of His New Testament ministry, of His Body, and of His testimony. Also, we need a clear and thorough vision concerning ourselves. We need to be exposed thoroughly. Our entire being needs to be opened up to the light to see where our heart is, where our mind is, where our will is, where our intention is, and where our motives are. We need to be so enlightened. Then we will be afraid to keep anything regional. I do not serve a few churches in my region. I serve the Lord's Body. If we were all here serving the Lord's Body, no local church would say that their meetings were better, higher, or more living than another locality. There would be no thought of telling other saints to come to your locality. You would consider that all the churches are the same as part of the Lord's Body.

Under His sovereignty, you are not assigned to take care of other churches. You have been assigned to take care of the churches in your region. You must realize, though, that these churches are not your churches but are the Lord's churches and are a part of His Body. If you had this kind of realization, you would never say that the meetings in your region are higher. You also would never tell anyone that if they are not satisfied with the situation in their region to please come to your region. In addition, you would never tell people not to go to another region because the churches there are not worth seeing. As long as you utter these kinds of words, this indicates that you only honor the churches in your region.

## Every Church Being Part of the Lord's Body

Every church is worth seeing because they are the churches of the Lord. These are the parts of His Body and they are worth seeing. Even the physical feet of the Lord Jesus were worthy of being loved by that sinful woman (Luke 7:37-38). She honored His two feet with her hair. The hair is the glory of a woman (1 Cor. 11:15), the top part of her body. With her top part she wiped the Savior's feet, the lowest part of His body, loving Him with her glory. Even His feet were worthy of her tears. In like manner, even the weakest churches are worth seeing because they are a part of His Body. If you did not have an improper, subconscious concept, you would never say that the churches in a certain region are not worth seeing. Also, you would never attempt to get people to move from other localities to your locality.

## No Church Being Our Church

We must learn to know our flesh. I want to impress you and I want it to remain in your memory that no church belongs to you or to me. The churches are God's churches, Christ's churches, and the saints' churches. No churches should be regional. All the churches should be catholic, universal. Strictly speaking, even the work you have done or are still doing is not your work. I do not consider what I am doing as my work. This is the Lord's work and I am just a small servant. By His mercy and grace He uses me to do certain things. This is not my work but His work. I am a slave of the Lord and a slave of you all. I am a slave even of all the weaker ones. I am not the master. I cannot say this is my work. The most I can say is that this is my service. Regardless of how much you have done and how wonderful what you have done is, remember that it is not your work. You should not keep what you have done in "your pocket" as your work. You should not hold what you have done all the time in your hand.

When I left Chefoo in 1944, nothing of the work or of the church was in "my pocket." Everything was in the hands of the brothers. In the same way, when I left Shanghai in 1949, Brother Nee sent a cable, and I went to the airlines to get my reservation. Three days later I took the plane and went away. Nothing in Shanghai was in my hands and I did not need to do anything. Also, when I left Los Angeles I never said a word to the brothers because nothing there was in my hands.

The leading brothers in Anaheim can testify that I do not know much about the church in Anaheim. I am just a brother attending the meetings. Sometimes, of course, the brothers would ask me about things and I would fellowship with them. This is all I do. Also, sometimes the brothers would pass on the financial statement to me. The Lord knows that I never read one. I leave it on my desk for a few days, and then it goes into the wastepaper basket. This does not mean that I was disgusted with that financial statement. This means that I do not consider that as my business. I do not want to know how much money the church in Anaheim receives and spends. This is not my business. This is why I have so much mental energy and time to concentrate myself on the holy Word. This is the main reason why I can do so much work. I do not scatter my mind or my energy to care for anything that is not within the limit of my responsibility.

## The Lord's Blessing and Our Usefulness

To serve the Lord and to be under His blessing is not a simple thing. Thank the Lord that the work, thus far, has been under His blessing. This is not due to me. This is due to His mercy which makes "this little servant" do his best to be pure and to be clean. The trouble among the Christians through the centuries has been impurity. Most Christians are doing good things. You cannot say that the Christians are doing bad things, but what about the purity? Whether or not you will be so useful in the Lord's hands for the long run and whether or not you will bring in the blessing for a lasting time does not depend on what you can do. It all depends on how pure your heart is. Therefore, ambition must be excluded and pride must be put under your feet. There should be no ambition, no thought for position, no pride, no self regard, and no self honor.

# CHAPTER FIVE

# PRINCIPLES FOR THE LEADING ONES AND THE WORKERS

The following fourteen points are crucial principles for the leading ones and the workers in the Lord's recovery.

## 1. BEARING THE TESTIMONY OF THE BODY OF CHRIST

A local church must bear the testimony of the Body of Christ. The Lord's recovery is for the testimony of the Body of Christ. This term, "the testimony of the Body of Christ," is all-embracing. A local church should not give people the impression that it bears a particular characteristic with a particular color or a particular flavor. Every local church must bear the testimony of the Body of Christ. We should not do anything particular. If we do anything particular, we will spoil the local churches' testimony. All the local churches should and must bear one unique testimony, that is, the testimony of Jesus which has become the testimony of the Body of Christ. We should endeavor by the Lord's mercy to delete, to reduce, and even to eliminate any particular characteristic, any particular flavor, or any particular color in your locality, in my locality, and in any other's locality. All the churches should just bear one unique characteristic, one particular color, and one particular flavor—the testimony of Jesus which is the testimony of the Body of Christ. If we would all take care of this, we would never do things which only fit in our local church. We must do things which fit in all the local churches and which would not damage or confuse the testimony of the Body of Christ.

## 2. BEING THE SAME AS THE OTHER CHURCHES

Do everything under the consideration of all the other churches, trying to be the same as the other churches. To do something merely under the consideration of the church in your locality which you are in is not adequate. It might be very good for your church, yet it may damage the testimony of the Body of Christ. Always try to be the same, not different. We all know that with the fallen human beings and in our human nature to be different from others is a pride, a boast, and a glory. Even in today's education there is a kind of promotion of this kind of boastful difference. However, we must consider that in the Lord's recovery to be different from the other churches is a shame and an insult to the Lord's recovery. We are the heavenly people, not the earthly people. For the earthly people to be different is for an earthly purpose and it is a boast and a glory. However, for the heavenly people and for God's heavenly purpose, God does not want and neither would He allow us to be different from others. He only has one move by one ministry to produce and build up one Body to bear one unique testimony. How then could we differ?

The children of Israel provide us with a good example. More than two million people traveled together, marched together, bore the same ark, and had the same tabernacle for their worship center. There was nothing different with them. According to the record or the revelation of the Old Testament type, difference is utterly prohibited. Anyone who would invent anything different, had to be cut off from God's people. It is a serious thing in God's eyes to make a difference because God has only one move. The type of the children of Israel shows us there is only one move by one ministry. In typology the Old Testament ministry carried out one thing—the tabernacle with the ark to bear one testimony which is God Himself mingled with His people.

To make a little difference in your local church from all the other churches is a serious thing. We can see an example of this by looking at our own physical body. If a doctor only cares for the arm of his patient, this care may damage the entire body. A good doctor or a surgeon never does things in this way. Whatever he does, he does it under the full consideration of the entire body. This is a proper doctor. Otherwise, you may think you are healing a person, but after two hours he dies because of your "healing." In like manner, in everything we do we must consider the entire Body. We must also consider what kind of impression we will leave to the Christians for the future.

### 3. NOT PROMOTING YOUR PLACE

Do not promote your place. If you promote your place, this means that you damage the entire recovery. If my arm would promote itself, it would become a "monster." This kind of promotion damages the entire body. The blood and cells of our body must go to every part of our body in proper proportions, but if we promote our place to draw people to our place, that means "the arm" draws more blood cells to itself. This damages the Body, and that particular part of the Body becomes diseased. Because the blood cells are going to the wrong place, this may cause a cancer in that place.

In the past, there has been a certain "promotion" in certain places. It may not have been done by the elders, but it was done by somebody. Otherwise, people would not have come to me. I never made this an issue, and I never considered it as an issue. I always, by the Lord's mercy, tried my best to calm down the ones who came to me. I charged them not to think in this way, but to go by the proper standing, and not to consider this as an issue. The fact that these ones came to me, however, showed that there was a "promotion" there.

We all must avoid this. Your locality may be the top locality. Let others say this, but you yourself should not say this. You should also watch over whether the saints in your locality are saying this. If they say this, charge them not to say it. This is sectarian. We are not here for any place, but we are here for the Lord's recovery. We are not here for American churches, Taiwan churches, Philippine churches, or European churches. We are here for the Lord's recovery as a whole Body. I hope that from now on no more information would come to us from certain saints questioning what is going on in a certain locality. Quite often it was very hard for me to answer these things. I could not justify this kind of promotion and neither would I be that unwise to condemn it before the reporters. If I did that, I would encourage the reporters to make an issue which would be a turmoil in the Lord's recovery. I would always do my best to calm the reporters down. They might have misunderstood that I was for that kind of promotion. However, I was not for that kind of promotion, and neither would I say any word to encourage the reporting ones to go ahead and talk about it. When this kind of information came to me, I was always put in a corner. It was very hard for me to answer because I cannot play politics and I cannot tell lies. Not only do I not control the churches, but also I always try the best to balance, to preserve, and to keep a calm situation between all the churches.

I beg you all to take care of this. This is not merely my own responsibility. This is our responsibility to keep a calm situation for the Lord's recovery to go on. If there is a turmoil, nothing can go on. A turmoil is like a storm that comes and the entire nation is stopped. Do not do this kind of thing. You may think this is a small thing, but actually it is not.

This principle we are discussing has two parts. The first part is not to promote your place, and the second part is not to catch people for your place. This has happened among us. Maybe this was not done by the leading ones, but by some of the saints in particular localities. They came out to promote your place and to ask people to go to your place saying that your place had the best church life. This has happened among us. Do not let this go on. This must be stopped. All the saints have their liberty and their right to stay in a locality or to move to another locality. Do not give advice as to where to go and as to where the church life is better or best. Never do this. In the eyes of the Lord all the churches are precious.

### 4. NOT ATTRACTING PEOPLE TO YOUR PLACE

Do not attract people to your place. When you go out to minister, to speak, to visit, or to have fellowship, do not exercise yourself in a way to attract people to you or to your place. We all should attract people to the Lord's recovery. We are not attracting people to our local church or to our work. We do not have our work. We only have the Lord's work. I do not have my local church. I only have the local churches of the Lord's recovery. Many of you can testify that I never directed people to come to Anaheim. Of course, people had to come to Los Angeles in the first ten years of the church life in the United States because that was nearly the only church with the ministry in the entire country. Today, however, the situation is different. Thank the Lord that the fishing net of the Lord's recovery is spread over the entire country and in every corner.

We should not practice in a way that attracts people to our place or to us instead of to the recovery. Let people appreciate the recovery more than your ministry and more than your doing. We are not here for our own work and we are not doing a piece of the so-called Christian work. We are all here bearing the ark and the ark was unique. There was only one tabernacle with only one ark, and today there is only one Christ and one universal church. We are now carrying this tabernacle with this ark. We are not the attracting center but the tabernacle with the ark is. Christ and the church—this should be the attracting center. We are not attracting people to our own work, to our place, or even to ourselves.

## 5. NOT SAYING THAT YOUR WAY IS BETTER

Do not say your way or what you do is better, even if your way is the best. I do not mean that you should not do things better. The church in Anaheim should try to do things better than the church in Cypress, and the church in Cypress should try to do things better than the church in Long Beach. This is very good, but do not fight. You do not need to designate or consider that your place is better. Probably your locality is not better. We do not need to say that we are better or that we have something better. Try your best to avoid this. This does not mean that you should not practice something better. Try to do something better as long as your doing does not damage the testimony of the Body. Your way might be improved, advanced, and better than all the other ways, yet you do not need to designate it as better, and you do not need to sell, promote, or talk about it. This always causes trouble. Do not say your way is improved and advanced. Do not say that others have deviated in a certain matter and that now you have an improved way. This kind of thing stirs troubling questions.

## 6. NOT MEASURING OTHER CHURCHES

Do not measure the other churches and especially do not measure people by your experience and by your way. Do not measure the churches by your way. It is very good not to measure and not to go to any place to measure.

## 7. NOT STIRRING UP THE CONCERN OF THE SAINTS

Always avoid doing anything or saying anything that would stir up the saints' concern for the Lord's recovery. A number of times information came to me that a certain brother did something or said something. This stirred up the saints' concern that this word or this kind of doing might damage the Lord's recovery. We should not do anything or say anything to stir up the faithful saints' concern for the Lord's recovery, causing them to think that we might be doing something to cause trouble. Sometimes their suspicion may even go further in causing them to think that what you said or did is a sign that you are going to rebel. When things such as this were reported to me by the concerned saints, I always did my best to quench this kind of suspicion. We must realize, however, that what was done and what was said produced this effect. You may not have done something or said something with that particular intention, but the negative effect still came out. Just because you did something innocently does not mean that the innocence is excusable. The fact that the damage has been done is what matters.

Most of the faithful saints are very sensitive because they love the recovery to the uttermost. Because they are very much for the recovery, they are constantly on the "watch-tower." When information came to me from these kinds of saints, eight out of ten times the information was correct. By the Lord's mercy, I would never take any information and believe in it. Every time the information came to me, the first thing I did was to calm down the other person. I always told them not to make an issue of this. I also told them not to talk to anyone from that time onward.

Again I say, try not to do things or say things that would stir up the faithful ones' concern. They are not only concerned for the Lord's recovery, but they are also concerned for you because they consider that you are so useful and that you are a real credit to the Lord's recovery. It would bother them to see you do something or say something which may not be for the one testimony. This would become a concern in their heart for you and for the Lord's recovery.

All of the information that ever has come to me in this kind of way was very carefully reported to me. The faithful saints who came to me with such information, came not in a careless or light way, but with very much consideration. At the beginning of 1978 I received some very long letters with detailed information concerning a troubling situation in a particular locality. In these letters the saints told me that they had considered this matter for a long time as to whether they should let me know about this situation. They told me that they had been for the Lord's recovery for over thirty years and had nearly sacrificed their lives to go this way. They indicated that they had also given their finances for the Lord's recovery and were absolutely for the migration to their particular locality. They said they had been watching the entire situation in their locality and after a certain amount of time they felt strongly that they must tell me. They also said that they felt that if they did not let me know about the matter, then they would not be faithful to the Lord.

After receiving these letters, I still would not believe the contents concerning this troubling situation. Yet I still considered. I never told anyone about this. I just kept this in my heart. Seemingly, I knew nothing because my intention was to let the fruit of this situation ripen by itself. Later, I was asked to go to this locality for the ministry of the Word. When I went and observed the situation there, I discovered that the letters I had received informed me of only twenty-five percent of the real situation there. The actual situation was seventy-five percent more than what these letters related to me.

This shows that there are some faithful ones in the Lord's recovery who have been with us all these years. The Lord's recovery is not "a new-born babe." It has been on this earth for sixty years. It came to the United States from the Far East, and a good number of faithful ones in the Far East came to this country. Also, some faithful ones were raised up in the United States, and these dear ones have put their life into the Lord's recovery. They are just for this. They are happy to see that you are so faithful and so useful. However, once they saw or heard something different, this concerned them very much. Your speaking and doing stirred up their concern. For example, when we went to the Far East in 1977, something was done which stirred up the real concern of the faithful ones in the Far East. Therefore, do not do anything or say anything that will stir up the faithful ones' concern for you and for the Lord's recovery. Always say something and do something to make the concerned ones feel peaceful.

## 8. NOT BEING SUSPICIOUS

On the other hand, do not be suspicious about others. We are not "ordained spies." All the spies learn to be suspicious and they would not believe anyone. I would even say to the faithful ones in the Lord's recovery that they should not learn to be spies. Learn to trust people. Your suspicion sometimes causes turmoil. Otherwise, we would now be in a "country of policemen." This is just like a communist country. Everywhere that we go we dare not say anything or do anything; otherwise, we would be caught. You must give people the liberty, the right, the freedom, the ease, and the peaceful feeling to say anything or do anything. Let people do things and do not be suspicious.

Truthfully speaking, some elders are suspicious all the time. They are suspicious of New York, Washington, D.C., Dallas, Anaheim, Miami, and other localities. You may feel that others may damage you or have an intention to put you out. You may also feel that even if such a thing is not present, at least the danger is there. We must realize, however, that we are in the Lord's hand and that we are under His hand. If you did not like to keep a position, you would not have to be so suspicious. If I do not want a position, I do not need to send out spies and I do not need to be suspicious about others. If the Lord wants me to work in this ministry, He does it through me. If the Lord wants me to be an elder, He does it. It is not up to me. This is why when information came to me, I did not look at the information first. I first looked at the informer's intention. In other words, I always ask why this person is reporting this matter to me. Even if something is being reported which is seemingly very much in my favor, I do not care for that. This is also a test. I always check the intention in the spirit of the reporter of this kind of information. In other words, what is behind your suspicion?

Let me relate a story to illustrate what I mean. In 1958 I went to visit England. We brothers in Taiwan firstly invited Brother T. Austin-Sparks to come to visit us in 1955. That was a marvelous time. Then we invited him to come a second time in 1957. At this time, Brother Sparks began to touch the matter of the church ground and did his best to annul this truth. During his two visits he invited me to visit them in England. Immediately after his second visit to Taiwan, there was turmoil in the churches in Taiwan. At least eight to ten saints were influenced by him. Therefore, I felt that I had to go to his place in London to see the real situation. Then I would have the ground to come back to render the help to these young influenced ones. Some of these young ones were even saved and raised up through my ministry.

I then wrote Brother Sparks and told him that I would come to visit him at his previous invitation. He answered my letter positively and he welcomed me. Despite his warm welcome, he checked with a British sister who had been with him for years—"Why is Brother Lee coming?" This shows that even with such a great minister who had a great ministry, politics was there. Do not think that what you do can be hidden. This British sister who had been close to Brother Sparks was actually closer to me at that time, and she told me that Brother Sparks checked with her as to my reason for going to see him. He was suspicious about my reason for going there. He was correct in thinking that there was a reason. However, the reason was not to undermine his work but to go to see what the real situation was there.

Human beings are human beings. If you have that much suspicion about so many things and about every one around you, this would cause others to consider why you are so suspicious. If you have no trust in people in the Lord's recovery, then I would surely begin to consider where you are. Therefore, do not be so suspicious.

Sometimes I was blamed for over trusting. Some saints said to me, "Brother Lee, the only problem with you is that you are over trusting. You trust in people too much." My children advised me not to trust that much. Sometimes I used Brother Nee's illustration concerning Judas. The Lord Jesus trusted in Judas. Did not the Lord know that Judas was stealing money from the money box (John 12:6)? The Lord was omniscient, yet He still trusted Judas. This is another principle—trust in people. Do not exercise suspicion.

## 9. WORKING AND CARING FOR THE LORD'S RECOVERY

Do not work and care for your local church or for the local churches in your territory, but for the Lord's recovery. Even if you are working in your territory for the recovery, your consideration should always be that you are working for the Lord's recovery. This will save us from much damage. Do not work only for your church, your territory. Do not care only for that territory. We all must work for the Lord's recovery. I speak this even to the local elders. The elders should not merely care or work for their locality but for the Lord's entire recovery.

## 10. NOT CUTTING YOURSELF OFF FROM THE BODY

Do not cut yourself off from the Body. If you cut one member off from the Body, this means that at least you cut yourself off from the Body. You must keep a very good fellowship with all the members in the Body. Do not think that because a certain one is not faithful to you or another one offended you, you would cut them off. Eventually, you cut yourself off from the Body. No person is perfect. People may offend you intentionally or unintentionally. Even if people offend you intentionally, you must learn to forgive, to forget, and to maintain a good fellowship.

The Lord Jesus told us in Matthew 5 that when we come to offer something to God, if we recall that someone is unhappy with us, we had better leave the offering there and get ourselves reconciled with the brother who has something against us (vv. 23-24). We are also told that to stumble or offend a brother is very serious in the Lord's eyes (Matt. 18:6-10). To cut off a member of the Body is also very serious. We should always, as much as possible, keep fellowship with everyone.

## 11. MINISTERING LIFE
## AND BUILDING UP THE CHURCHES

Minister life wherever you go, and build up the churches wherever you are. Do not do or say anything negative. Wherever you go, minister life in a positive way. Wherever you are, build up the church positively.

## 12. CONSIDERING THE CHURCHES,
## THE CO-WORKERS, AND THE SAINTS THE SAME

Consider all the churches, all the co-workers, and all the saints the same. Do not consider that those who are with you are superior. All the churches, all the co-workers on this earth, and all the saints on this globe universally should be the same in our consideration.

## 13. NOT HAVING A SPECIAL GROUP

Do not build a special group around you. By the Lord's mercy, I can boast that I do not have any "buddies." I do not have a special group around me. Instead, I probably have offended many of you. Many of you know that the closer you are to me, the more frank speaking you get from me.

Some among you, however, whether intentionally or unintentionally have a group around you. For the long run, and for the Lord's profit, interest, and for His recovery, this is not a credit to you. I can always boast that I have hundreds of co-workers, but I do not have a special group around me. I do not know who is closer to me today. Actually, everybody is closer. The betrayers always consider that they are the closest. The

principle is there with Judas. He was very close, and he
betrayed the Lord Jesus with a kiss. Peter did not do something to show people that he was so close to the Lord Jesus.
The principle is the same today. Please widen your scope.
Every saint in the Lord's recovery is your help.

## 14. NOT TRYING TO CONVINCE OTHERS THAT YOUR WAY IS THE BEST

Do not try to convince others that your way is the best.
This is similar to item number five which says not to say that
your way is the right way. Sometimes certain ones not only
said that their way was the right or the best way, but tried to
convince others of this. This spontaneously and immediately
caused a turmoil. This turmoil damaged them, damaged
others, and eventually damaged the Lord's recovery. I believe
that we all love the Lord, and that we all love the Lord's
recovery. The Lord's recovery may be considered as our babe.
Just as a mother loves her babe, so we have to love our babe.
We must sacrifice our everything for this babe. This is the
conclusion of my fellowship on these principles. Do not do
anything or say anything that would damage the Lord's
recovery.

CHAPTER SIX

# THE RECEIVING OF THE SAINTS

## (1)

### RECEIVING ALL THE BELIEVERS

How we receive all the saints determines whether or not we are a sect. Merely to say that we are standing on the ground of oneness is not adequate. We should stand on the ground of oneness, yet we must have some governing conditions and terms. The first governing condition is how to receive the saints. In principle, we must receive all of the saints. This is fully covered by the Apostle Paul in Romans 14 and 15. Paul tells us that we have to receive all kinds of believers (surely he means the real believers) who may be different from us. Even if there are believers that still keep the Sabbath and that still eat the Jewish religious diet, there is no ground for us to reject them. If we reject them, we become a sect.

One of the basic constituents by which any group of Christians is constituted to be a denomination is that they only receive the saints according to their kind of taste or their kind of belief. The Southern Baptists insist on baptism by immersion. With them, you even have to be baptized by immersion in their water. If you are baptized by others in others' water, they do not recognize this. This is a strong sect with millions of members. Their numbers, however, do not justify them. Numbers do not justify anyone, but their practice does. We have to receive everyone whom Christ has received (Rom. 15:7).

## Practicing According to the Proper Principle and According to God's Love

Some may say that we have to receive the genuine believers because some believers are not genuine. We have to be very careful, however, in saying this. We must realize that we cannot discern things to a full extent. It is true that we only receive the genuine believers, but we may make a mistake in this matter of discerning who is a genuine believer.

For example, here is a person who prays and says he believes in the Lord Jesus, yet to your feeling this one has not been genuinely regenerated. Therefore, you would insist on keeping the principle that we only receive the genuine believers. The three other elders whom you coordinate with, though, may feel that this man is saved because he believes in the Lord Jesus, he confesses his sins, and he prays to the Lord. To make a decision in this case by voting surely is not the way. We must learn two things: first, to keep the principle of receiving the genuine believers, and second, not to trust that any single person's feeling is one hundred percent right; we must practice the principle of the Body to have at least two or three to make the final decision by exercising their spirit (1 Cor. 2:14-15).

A certain person, according to your feeling, might not be genuinely regenerated, yet he may be truly regenerated in fact. None of us should be overconfident to insist on his own feeling. When all of us are not sure in our feeling concerning the genuineness of anyone's regeneration, we should make a positive decision according to God's love, as long as this one assures us that he believes in the Lord Jesus, confesses his sins, and prays to the Lord. According to my experience over the years, when we practiced according to God's love in receiving ones concerning whom we dare not say definitely whether or not they are truly regenerated, our receiving was right most of the time. Such persons sometimes became very good brothers.

## Denying Our Disposition

I may be a person living in my particular nature and in my peculiar disposition, which is always so straight and so insistent. I am very strict about not receiving anyone whom I feel is not genuinely regenerated. I think I am keeping the proper principle, but actually I am keeping my peculiar disposition. Do not practice your disposition. You must practice God's nature, not your nature.

To receive people you must keep in mind three things: 1) the proper principle of receiving the saints; 2) not being overconfident in your feeling; and 3) not being according to your disposition but according to God's nature of love. To receive people whom you are not sure whether or not they are truly regenerated is safer than not to receive them. If you do not receive them, you may miss them. Some of the ones that you do not receive may eventually be very useful to the Lord. You may appreciate a certain one and you would receive him immediately. After some time, however, he might become a problem to you. Who can tell? We must go the safer way of receiving people. This does not mean, however, that we receive whoever comes to us. They must believe in the Lord Jesus. They have to confess the Lord's name, As long as they believe in the Lord Jesus, and confess their sins, do not demand more of them. Do not practice any principle according to your kind of taste which actually is not your taste, but your peculiarity. That is your particular and peculiar disposition. We must deny our disposition in receiving the saints.

## LOSING THE FELLOWSHIP OF THE CHURCH

At this point, I would like to study with you a number of portions of the Word which deal with the matter of a believer losing the fellowship of the church.

### Matthew 18:15-17

The first portion concerning this matter is in Matthew 18:15-17: "Now if your brother sins, go, reprove him between you and him alone. If he hears you, you have gained your brother. But if he does not hear you, take with you one or two more, that by the mouth of two or three witnesses every word may be established. But if he refuses to hear them, tell it to the church; and if he refuses to hear the church also, let him be to you as the Gentile and the tax collector." If one brother sins, we should not expose him, but "reprove him between you and him alone." If he does not hear you, you should not spread the thing to many, but just to one or two among us. If this brother refuses to hear you and the other one or two, you should tell it to the church. This is crucial and this is the last step.

If this brother refuses to hear the church, the Lord Jesus tells us to "let him be." These three words, "let him be," comprise a crucial point for us to interpret. "Let him be" is an interpretation of one Greek word. This Greek word is not a strong word and does not mean cut him off, cast him out, or put him aside. Even to "consider him" as a Gentile is stronger than the original text. When we exercise to understand the holy Word, especially to interpret it, we should not do it lightly. We must be like a lawyer understanding and interpreting the law. We cannot do it carelessly since this is not the human law but the constitution of the kingdom of the heavens in Matthew. According to the Greek in verse 17 the meaning is to "let him be what he is." This means to look on him as a Gentile losing the fellowship. This matter is up to him. It is not your doing nor is it the elders' doing.

Some have argued with me concerning the interpretation of this verse. They understood that this verse meant to excommunicate him. The Lord Jesus here, however, does not mean that. Even though a certain brother may not be directly offending you, this brother sins. You should go to him in love to recover him. Eventually, however, you must bring his case to the church. If this one would still refuse to listen, should you excommunicate him? No. Let him be to you as one who loses, who misses, the fellowship as a Gentile and as a tax collector. Note 17[3] in Matthew 18 (Recovery Version) says, "If any believer refuses to hear the church, he will lose the fellowship of the church like the Gentile, the heathen, and the tax collector, the sinners who are outside the fellowship of the church." In other words, this matter is up to him. He loses the fellowship. This is not for you to cut him off. We must be careful. We must realize that to cut a saint off from the church is a tremendously serious matter.

If we cut off people from the church, we do not value the

church fellowship properly. If we treasure the church fellowship highly, we would not cut people off from this fellowship, because it is so high. To cut off people so easily and so broadly means that we do not treasure the fellowship and that we do not value the fellowship properly. If you possess a treasure of tremendous value, you should handle it very carefully. It is easy, however, to cut off something cheap. When we cut off something easily, this means that we do not treasure that item and that we deal with it cheaply. The church fellowship is precious beyond measure. We should not keep anyone out of this fellowship lightly. We must be careful.

## Romans 16:17-18

Romans 16:17-18 says, "Now I beg you, brothers, keep a watchful eye on those who make divisions and causes of falling contrary to the teaching which you have learned, and turn away from them. For such men do not serve as slaves our Lord Christ, but their own appetites; and by smooth and flattering speech deceive the hearts of the simple." These ones even make divisions and causes of falling contrary to the teachings which we have heard, teachings, which, no doubt, are the ministry of the New Testament economy. This is a very serious matter, yet Paul still did not tell us to cut off such ones. The most we can do is to turn away from them. Maybe we can also render some advice to them in love. Whether or not they would listen is up to them, but we should not go further than this.

## Titus 3:10

Titus 3:10 says, "A factious man after a first and second admonition refuse." A factious man is a sectarian man, a man making divisions. Concerning this verse note $10^2$ in the Recovery Version says, "In order to maintain good order in the church, a factious, divisive person, after a first and second admonition, should be refused, rejected. This is to stop intercourse with a contagiously divisive person for the church's profit." Paul still did not say, however, to excommunicate such a person. We have to be very careful not to interpret this case as a case of excommunication. To reject does not go as far as to cast away.

## Third John 9-10

Third John 9-10 says, "I wrote something to the church, but Diotrephes, who loves to be first among them, does not receive us. Therefore, if I come, I will bring to remembrance his works which he does, babbling against us with evil words; and not being satisfied with these, neither does he receive the brothers, and those intending to do so he forbids and casts them out of the church." This situation was very serious because Diotrephes himself was casting brothers out from the church. However, John did not tell the saints that they had to make a decision to cast Diotrephes out, although he was casting out people.

## Second John 10

Second John 10 says, "If anyone comes to you and does not bring this teaching, do not receive him into your house, and do not say to him, Rejoice!" The teaching referred to in verse 10 is "the teaching of Christ" in verse 9 which is the truth concerning the deity of Christ, especially regarding His incarnation by divine conception (1 John 4:2). "Everyone who goes beyond and does not abide in the teaching of Christ, does not have God; he who abides in the teaching, this one has both the Father and the Son" (v. 9). If anyone comes to us and does not bring this teaching concerning Christ's deity, do not receive him into your house and do not say rejoice to him; do riot greet him. In this particular case, we should not greet such a one, we should not receive him into our house, and we surely should not receive him to the church meeting.

## First Corinthians 5:9-13

First Corinthians 5:9-13 is the strongest passage concerning removing someone from the fellowship of the church: "I wrote to you in the letter not to associate with fornicators, not altogether with the fornicators of this world, or with the avaricious and rapacious, or idolaters, since then you would have to go out of the world. But now I have written to you not to

associate with anyone who is called a brother, if he is a forni-
cator or an avaricious man or an idolater or a reviler or a
drunkard or a rapacious man; with such a one not even to eat.
For what have I to do with judging those who are without? Do
you not judge those who are within? But those who are without God judges. Remove the evil man from among yourselves."
This is a clear case of removing, cutting off, an evil man from
the fellowship of the church.

### First Timothy 1:20 and Second Timothy 4:14

The case of Alexander the coppersmith is recorded in
1 Timothy 1:20 and 2 Timothy 4:14. Alexander was one who
attacked and opposed the Apostle Paul to the uttermost. Of
course, such a one should not be taken into the church life.
All these Scriptures present cases which we have to consider
in our fellowship concerning receiving the saints. We should
not remove, cut off, someone from the fellowship of the church
in a light manner, but we must do it carefully.

#### REMOVING SOMEONE
#### FROM THE FELLOWSHIP OF THE CHURCH

To stop a saint from coming to the Lord's table should not
be done unless it is a case related to immorality, to idol worship, or to the heresy concerning the Lord's Person. Suppose a
person does not believe that the Lord is the Son of God. Neither does he believe that Jesus is God. We should not allow
such a person to come to the Lord's table. One may ask why
we do not excommunicate an immoral person and only stop
him from coming to the Lord's table. We must realize that the
matter of so-called excommunication involves families and
people's name in society. To remove someone from the fellowship of the church is a great matter, so we should not do this
too quickly but, rather, carefully. Also, we want to give people
a time for repentance.

For example, there may be a case in a locality of a person
who commits fornication. It is not wise to immediately cut
this one off from the fellowship of the church. They should,
however, be told to stop coming to the Lord's table because of
their immorality. We should also warn them to repent and to

clear up the matter so that we can cover the matter in love to rescue the involved persons and families. On the one hand, we would not let them come to the Lord's table. On the other hand, we would cover them which means to protect them. We protect them by giving them a chance to repent and clear up the situation. Eventually, if they would still continue to live in that sin and if there were no indication or sign that they would leave that sin and repent to give up their immorality, this would force the church to cut off the fellowship with them.

Again, to remove a person from the fellowship of the church should not be carried out in a fast way. We must consider the possible damages which can be done by doing something of this nature in a fast and careless way. We saw things in the past that happened outside of us in other Christian groups. This kind of thing caused the breaking up of families and even suicide in some cases. We have to be careful about these things. Even the law does not give the liberty to the church pastor to expose people's sin in this way because they must take care of their family.

For example, if a young wife were to commit fornication with another man and if this were exposed and made known to her husband and relatives, this would cause a great turmoil. To deal with this matter needs much wisdom. As long as a person expresses repentance and you cannot say he has not really repented, you must take him. If he goes back to the same sin after you have taken him, you must stop him again. Then after a certain time, he may come back to express his repentance and you must take him again. After a while, however, he may go back to his old sin and you must stop him again. We must consider all this and not do anything hastily.

We always must practice anything that concerns the church life in love. We receive people in love. Even if we put out people when it is necessary, we do this also in love. For example, we may not be sure whether a certain new one among us is saved or not. We have to keep the divine principle that only the saved ones can join the church and participate in the Lord's table. Here is a person, however, whom we cannot say is definitely saved. It is hard to say, either, that he is not saved. In a case like this, we must practice the principle in love. If we do not have the assurance that he is not saved, we should not reject him. We must say, "Lord, I am not too clear. According to Your loving heart, I do not have the boldness to reject this one. Lord, I take him under Your love. If I am wrong, Your blood cleanses me. Have mercy upon this person." According to our experiences in the past, most of these cases are positive and the Lord honors this. If we are so clear that a person is not saved, we should deliberately yet nicely tell him that he had better wait to partake of the Lord's table. We would still encourage him to come to the meetings and to listen to the truth to hear the gospel. We should tell him to wait, yet we should still encourage him to keep coming.

If you do not have the assurance and clarity that the removing of someone from the fellowship will not damage any party, do not carry it out in an exposing way. This is also in love. This does not mean that we overlook these immoralities. Rather, we are wholly for the Lord and we want to keep the church free from any immorality. We also want to keep the Lord's table from being contaminated with any immoral person. To practice this, however, we must consider people's humanity and their involvement in society. There are husbands, children, wives, parents, relatives, and in-laws to consider. This is why we must be so careful.

Of course, if a person is not really immoral, we should not put him out. Once we put him out, this putting out may put a mark upon him that he really is immoral. Then the society will believe him to be an immoral person. This is something quite serious. Sometimes a person may rebel against the church and sue the church because you damaged his name. Do not think this could not happen. We must be careful even to protect the church legally.

We must carry out everything we do in love. To love is always right. However, if you put out people to keep your position and rank as an elder, this is altogether not in love. You are just putting out people as a cloak of protecting your position and your rank. This is wrong. We must practice the church life according to justice in love. This is exactly what the Lord does. Do not think that to require a public repentance is so right because any sin is contagious. It is always better to cover sin. This does not mean that the church is immoral, unclean, or unholy in covering sinful things.

## PUBLIC CONFESSION

Fifty years ago in China, some in the Pentecostal movement required and instigated the public confession of sins. Some of these public confessions issued in suicide, fighting, and turmoil in the society, which nearly caused the government to stop such a thing. This shows us that we should not dig out all these sinful things. We should do our best to help individuals make a clear confession before the Lord. Even the so-called confession to the priests in the Catholic Church has caused much trouble. The man who is considered the father of the Republic of the Philippines confessed to a Catholic priest that he did something to revolt against the Spanish government. This priest then passed on this information to the government, and the government arrested him and put him to death.

These examples again show us that we must handle these matters very carefully. Even if a person volunteers to make a public confession, we had better advise him not to do it. This does not edify anyone. These are dirty things to dirty our ears and to dirty the minds of the young people. Once you hear things like this, it will be hard for you to forget them for the rest of your life. This is not so healthy.

The ones who are for the public confessions of sins use two portions of the Scriptures as their basis. They say that when people were baptized by John in the Jordan River they confessed their sins (Matt. 3:6), and also that the ones who believed in Acts 19 confessed their sins and made known their practices (v. 18). We must realize, however, that these are spontaneous cases and not teachings which require you to do this.

## A LIMIT OF PUNISHMENT

Something divisive which has happened and which has been manifested to everybody does not involve people's morality in principle. Even if we said something concerning this,

this would not constitute any kind of defamation, and this would not be contagious to the listening ears. Even with the matter of divisiveness, however, we must take care of it in a very careful way. According to the Old Testament law, when a sinful brother is going to be punished with forty stripes, this punishment had better be done with thirty-nine stripes (Deut. 25:1-3; 2 Cor. 11:24). Thirty-nine lashes were given in order to insure that the limit of forty was not exceeded. There is the possibility of meting out more punishment than is necessary because there is something in us which likes to punish people. When we punish, we punish more than is needed. Even in dealing with our children, we should not forget the principle of thirty-nine stripes rather than forty. This principle is to safeguard us from over punishing someone. Therefore, we should always under punish. If you have a burden to give a certain saint forty dollars in love, you had better give him forty-one dollars. To love more is safe. To punish more is not safe. We must see the principle in the Word.

## CONSIDERING THE OTHER CHURCHES

Also, when you consider putting out or cutting off a saint from the fellowship of the church you must consider what the other churches will do. Once you have thoroughly considered that you have no choice that a certain one has to be put out, then you must put him out. When such a person comes to the other churches they must consider whether or not to receive him back since he was cut off from the fellowship in another locality. When we receive such a one, we must receive him with much consideration for the other churches. In doing anything we must do it under the consideration of the other churches. If we receive someone, can the other churches receive this one? If we put out someone, will all the other churches agree with us to put this certain one out? If we deal with these matters in this way, we will be protected and, at least, we will be balanced. We will not go too far.

## ALEXANDER THE COPPERSMITH

I do not think we need to consider the case of Alexander the coppersmith as a case of so-called excommunication. He was one who was attacking the apostle and damaging the ministry. Since he was an enemy and an opponent already, there was no need to cut him off from the fellowship of the church. When a person speaks negatively about the ministry, you should not consider that as an attack. We must give people the liberty to express what they feel and think. However, I believe Alexander the coppersmith went much farther than this. Otherwise, Paul would not have said such a strong word about him. To criticize the ministry, to say something bad about the ministry, and even to oppose the ministry should not be considered as the type of attacking that was done by Alexander the coppersmith.

In conclusion, I say again that we must always remember that when we practice anything for justice, we must do it in love. We must also reduce the extent and the quantity of the punishment from "forty stripes to thirty-nine." This is safe.

CHAPTER SEVEN

# THE RECEIVING OF THE SAINTS

## (2)

### SECOND THESSALONIANS 3:14-15

In the previous chapter, we studied portions of Scripture concerning the matter of cutting a saint off from the fellowship of the church. Second Thessalonians 3:14-15 is another portion of Scripture related to this matter. "If anyone does not obey our word by this letter, mark this one that you may not associate with him, in order that he may be put to shame; and do not count him as an enemy, but admonish him as a brother." Seemingly, Paul's words in these two verses are contradictory. In verse 14 Paul says that you may not associate with him. According to our understanding this means not to contact him, but in verse 15 Paul says to admonish him as a brother. How can these two verses be reconciled?

According to our natural understanding, Paul charged us to reject this person because he says that we may not associate with him, which to us means that we should have nothing to do with him. The second verse, however, tells us that we must admonish him as a brother. Although we may not associate with him, this does not mean that we should not contact him. This means we should not associate with him as a companion. We should not count him as an enemy or give him up but admonish him.

### FIRST CORINTHIANS 5:13

The strongest portion of the Word that we have looked at concerning the matter of cutting off a saint from the fellowship of the church is in 1 Corinthians 5:13 which says,

"Remove the evil man from among yourselves." Most Christian teachers interpret the word "remove" as meaning to excommunicate. Actually, there is no excommunication here. Paul uses the word "remove." The fact that this is not a case of excommunication is also fully proven by Paul's second Epistle to the Corinthians, The Apostle Paul told us that after he wrote the first Epistle, he regretted that his charge was too strong (2 Cor. 7:8). In addition, this brother who was condemned, repented, so Paul wrote a second letter, asking the church in Corinth to forgive this brother, to receive him, and to love him (2:5-10). Paul charged the saints there not to reject this brother at all; otherwise, Satan would have the ground to come in to the situation (2:11). Second Corinthians proves that what Paul charged in 1 Corinthians 5 was not an excommunication. Merely according to Paul's own word in 1 Corinthians 5, to remove this evil one does not constitute a kind of excommunication. First, the word "remove" is not a legal term. All Paul says is to remove him. If this were a legislative matter, the word excommunicate might be used. Paul, however, did not use such a word. This shows us that our understanding concerning this matter should be reconsidered. All the leading ones who bear the responsibility for the Lord's testimony of the churches must consider this because to deal with a brother is not a small thing. We need to study our constitution, which is the New Testament.

### MATTHEW 18:17

We have already seen that in Matthew 18:17 the Lord Jesus only used the word "let him be." Matthew 18 shows us that we must do our best to fellowship with a sinning brother. If he would not take our word, we should bring one or two brothers to help him. If he still would not listen to them, then this case should be referred to the church. If he still would not listen to the church, then what should we do? Should we throw him out and forget about him? The Lord's word is to "let him be." Let him be to you as a heathen and a tax collector. This matter is up to him. The Lord's expression is very careful.

The foregoing verses in chapter 18 show us the reason why the Lord is so careful. In this foregoing portion, the Lord warns us that to stumble a little one is a serious matter (18:6). Matthew 18 is a chapter on the proper dealings with our fellow believers, our brothers. We must be careful. The Lord Jesus charges us firstly in Matthew 18 not to stumble "one of these little ones who believe in Me" (v. 6). To stumble a little one is a serious matter, yet this one may be sinful and may have just committed a sin. When you are going to deal with him, be careful. Do not stumble a sinful brother by your dealing with him. If your dealing with him is not proper, this dealing may stumble him for his whole life. Then who is responsible for this? Yes he was sinful, but you did not deal with him properly. Your wrong dealing stumbled him. With a proper dealing he might have been brought to the Lord. You might have had a good intention in your dealing with him, but the issue was his being stumbled.

## NO NEED OF A PUBLIC ANNOUNCEMENT

Unconsciously we are still under the influence of the traditions of Christianity which are hidden in many aspects of our practice of the church life. This matter of excommunication comes from tradition. Also, we have always considered the proper time to make an announcement of a certain excommunication. We thought a public announcement was needed, but there is no hint in the New Testament that we need to make a public announcement. Even in 1 Corinthians 5, Paul did not say that the saints there had to make a public announcement. He only charged the church to remove the sinful brother.

In the past, we all thought there was the need of making a public announcement. We must see, however, that to make a public announcement of a kind of excommunication involves a person's name, position, and status in today's society. This is serious and very risky. This involves families and human relationships. In this matter we have been under the influence of the tradition of Christianity, but in my experiences over the past fifty years I have surely learned that to make a public announcement, especially in a matter concerning immorality, is not so safe and profitable. If we announce a certain person's being excommunicated in a public meeting, he could appeal to a court of law and say that we are spoiling his name. He would claim that since you said he committed immorality, you must provide the evidence in a court of law. This would cause much trouble. This one may have committed that sin, but according to law you must present the evidence. This sinning one may not have that much growth in the Lord, but he may bold a high position in society. He would vindicate himself by bringing this case to the law court to clear up his name. This shows us the turmoil that such a public announcement could cause. Also, such a public announcement could damage families. This could also cause a young female to have no way to go on, humanly speaking, and no way to live, especially in the Far East.

According to our present knowledge of the New Testament, I do not believe there is the need of making a public announcement. We just need to tell the sinning one, "We have been waiting for your repentance and, thus far, we could not see it. Since you know the Lord is holy and His table is holy, please stay away, not only from the Lord's table but also from the church meetings." This kind of fellowship is sufficient. If we know that this one is still contacting certain brothers and sisters, we may pray to seek the Lord's wisdom concerning how to handle the situation and how to let the involved parties know. We must do things in this wise way with love, and we must be careful. In this matter there is a social element involved, so there is also a legal element involved. There is always some possibility that a person could bring the church to the law court.

### AVOIDING USING THE WORD "EXCOMMUNICATION"

Also, I feel that we had better avoid using the word "excommunication" because we must leave the ground, the opening, for the sinning one to come back. If we use the word excommunicate, this is too strong. This may close the door to the sinning one. We should remember that when we need to give "forty stripes" we should only give thirty-nine (Deut. 25:3). Never punish someone over the limit. Try your best to punish less.

## THE DESCENDANTS OF KORAH

During my study of 1 Samuel, I discovered that Samuel's ancestor was Korah. First Chronicles 6:33 says, "And these are they that waited, and their sons. Of the sons of the Kohathites: Heman the singer, the son of Joel, the son of Samuel" (ASV). The Kohathites were descendants of Levi (1 Chron. 6:1). Samuel was the grandfather of Heman, who was a musician under David the king. The title of Psalm 88 reads, "A Song or Psalm for the sons of Korah, to the chief Musician upon Mahalath Leannoth, Maschil of Heman the Ezrahite." Heman was the chief musician and I believe more than one song was sung to his melody. David selected Heman to be the leader of the songs. He should have been a very devoted person, and he was a grandson of Samuel and a descendant of Korah. First Chronicles 6:37 says, "The son of Tahath, the son of Assir, the son of Ebiasaph, the son of Korah." This tells us that not only Heman but also Samuel were descendants of the rebellious Korah (Num. 16:1-50). When I first began to study the Bible, I thought the entire family of Korah was all swallowed up by the earth. However, the further record of the Old Testament shows that there were some escapees (Num. 26:9-11). The sons of Korah are referred to in the titles of many Psalms (42, 44—49, 84—85, 87—88). Even from the rebellious family of Korah there came descendants who composed such godly songs. Also, the great prophet, Samuel, was a descendant of Korah. All of us condemn Korah as a rebellious one, but God's mercy is still present. Out of this rebellious family came the greatest prophet who turned the age into the age of the kingdom with the kingship—Samuel. This again shows us that we must be careful in dealing with a sinful one. We need to exercise at least a small amount of the mercy of God and leave some opening for the "escapees."

## THE LABOR OF LIFE AND IN LOVE

Do not deal with others or discipline them absolutely. You must love others absolutely, but to deal with others in a manner of discipline is a matter which requires "thirty-nine

stripes" and not forty. Micah 6:6-8 indicates that God cares
for mercy. The Lord Jesus also says in Matthew 9:13, "I desire
mercy and not sacrifice." This does not mean that we are
loose in the matter of immorality. We are not loose, but we
have to labor.

Once there is a sinful case in the church life, we should not
let it go loosely. We have to deal with it by much labor of life.
The tendency in our practice is either not to take care of the
matter or to take care of it in a hurry. The Bible shows,
though, that we must deal with this thing carefully. This is
like a good doctor who uses his skill to heal a dying patient.
He has to labor on this patient bit by bit. Paul labored in such
a way in writing 1 Corinthians and labored again to deal
with this sinning brother in writing 2 Corinthians. We have to
learn of Paul not to deal with a sinful case in a brief, quick
way. We must labor in love. We have to take care of a sinful member in the church in love and deal with him with
wisdom, hoping that he could be helped to repent to come back
to the Lord. We have to minister life to him to help him receive
the life supply that he may regain his lost fellowship with the
Lord.

## BY WISDOM, WITH PATIENCE, AND IN LOVE

For the entire testimony of the Lord on this earth, we
must learn to carry out the same ministry and to speak the
same thing. Then concerning the sinful cases in the local
churches, we must deal with them by wisdom, with patience,
and altogether in love. We love even the sinful members, so
we deal with them in love. For God's holiness, God's righteousness, and even for the church's testimony, we must deal
with the sinful member, yet our dealing should be by wisdom,
with patience, and in love.

For all of us to be healthy for the Lord's recovery, we need
to take care of two points—the major point of bearing the
same testimony and the small point of dealing with a sinful
brother with wisdom in love. The principle is "with wisdom in
love." This must be the atmosphere in the church. We love not
only the good ones but also the sinful ones. This, however,
does not mean that we are light or loose. We are very strict,

yet we carry out such dealings with patience, with much wisdom, and in love. We must receive the saints properly in our locality so that all the local churches can go along with us. Our receiving of the saints should in no way be sectarian. Then in dealing with the saints, we deal with the cases with wisdom in love, and do not give Satan an advantage. We should not close the door for the sinning one to be recovered, and we should not do anything without love.

# CHAPTER EIGHT

# THE POSITION AND FUNCTION
# OF THE ELDERS

## THE POSITION OF THE ELDERS

In this chapter we will have a thorough fellowship concerning the elders' position and function. How a church goes on depends upon the eldership. We cannot say that there is absolutely no position of elders. Actually, any person has a position. Even a man or a child has a position. The professors have a position in their schools and even a student has his position. We all must see this matter of the position of the elders.

## No Rank

First, the position of the elders should not be considered a position of any high rank. Strictly speaking, according to the New Testament, in the church there should be no rank. This matter of ambition for position and rank was there even with the early disciples, especially among the twelve (Matt. 20:20-24). In Matthew 20 and 23 the Lord Jesus did not allow one inch of ground to be given to rank. He told the disciples that the church was not like the Gentiles. With the Gentiles there are kings and persons of high rank to govern them, but there should be nothing like this among the believers. Then the Lord Jesus said, "And whoever wants to be first among you shall be your slave" (Matt. 20:27). Among the believers there is only the brotherhood; we are all brothers (Matt. 23:8).

When the Brethren were raised up in Britain, many people did their best to ascribe a name to them so that they could be denominated. Because people could not find a name

for them, they began to call them the Brethren because they
practiced the fact in the Bible that they were all brothers
without rank. The name that was used was the King James
rendering "brethren." This was not a name that the brothers
picked up themselves. Rather, it was a nickname ascribed to
them. They realized that there should be no rank among the
believers.

Also, before the so-called Plymouth Brethren there were
brothers in the seventeenth century known as the Grace
Brethren and the Moravian Brethren. There were different
kinds of brothers in Europe which followed the principle that
among the believers there should be no rank. We all have a
position, but do not think that we have a rank.

Then the episcopal thought invaded the church. Episcopal
means having the church government by bishops. The word
bishop is included in the word episcopal which in the Greek
is *episkopos*. It was Ignatius in the second century who mistakenly taught that an overseer, a bishop, is higher than an
elder. However, an overseer (or bishop) in a local church is
an elder (Acts 20:17, 28). The two titles refer to the same
person; elder denoting a person of maturity; overseer, denoting the function of an elder. An elder is a brother who is more
mature and more experienced. This does not denote any rank.
To interpret in this way is according to the worldly, natural
concept. When the word overseer is used, most people do not
have the concept that this is a high rank. However, the word
bishop (from Latin *episcopus*) carries with it the concept of a
high rank in the religious mind. Today in Catholicism there is
the hierarchy of bishops, archbishops, cardinals, and the
pope. The degraded and organized Christianity has brought
in the concept of rank and is using terms such as these. Not
only do the Catholic Church and the Episcopal Church have
bishops, but also the Methodists have bishops. Ignatius was a
dear brother, but he made a big mistake in teaching that an
overseer, a bishop, was higher than an elder. This shows us
that we must be careful in interpreting the Bible. An overseer
or bishop according to Ignatius controls the elders in the
churches. This may have seemed like a small mistake, but

this was the opening of the door for the hierarchy in today's Christendom.

We must realize that this thought of rank still remains in our mentality. This thought is not only devilish but, even more, it is hellish. We must got rid of this thought of rank. It should not remain in our mentality. Everybody has a position. The sisters have their position and the brothers have their position, but there should be no rank. The elders are not higher than the brothers and the sisters in the local church. Rather, according to the Lord's teaching, the elders are lower because they are the slaves. The sisters who are the wives of the elders should not consider that their husband is higher than others. They should consider that their husbands are slaves and that they are the wives of the slaves. On the other hand, we consider that it is a real honor to be a slave to serve the churches.

## Shepherding the Flock of God

If we would drop the concept concerning rank, it would be easy for us to understand the matter of position. If rank is gone, the position means nothing. Actually, I would say, strictly speaking, that the elders should not consider that they have any position. They have no position. The Apostle Peter could not forget the Lord's teaching concerning this matter. In his first Epistle Peter told the elders as a "fellow-elder" (5:1) not to lord it over the brothers and the sisters but to be a living example, a pattern (v. 3).

According to the actual situation of a shepherd and a flock, the shepherd, strictly speaking, cannot be an example to the flock. The shepherd is a man and the flock is cattle. How can a man be an example to cattle? Actually, though, the flock as the church is a composition of men. The saints are not cattle, but they are men just as the elders are men. The elders are men, but they are also the shepherds. They should not shepherd a flock of men as they would a flock of cattle. The elders have to shepherd the "man flock" by setting themselves up, the living men, as examples. Whatever the saints in the local church should do or live, the elders must do it and live it first. Then their doing and their living will be a living example. This is the way to shepherd. According to this way, the elders do not have a rank nor do they have a position. If they do have a position, their position is the same as all the saints.

In God's economy, the shepherd and the flock all are men and all of them should be the same because the shepherd should be an example. If the shepherds, the elders, are extraordinary, different people, they could never be examples to others. Since they can be examples to others, they are the same as others. For instance, we cannot say that the king should be an example to the civilians. We also cannot say that the governor of a state should be an example to the citizens of this state. However, Peter says as an elder that all the elders should be living examples of the flock.

## No Control

Also, according to the Lord's word in the Gospels and to Peter's words in his Epistle, the holy Word does not allow the elder to control at all. The Lord Jesus stressed this point very strongly. The leading ones should not be rulers, but slaves, servants, who serve and who do not control. Then Peter tells the elders not to lord it over the believers. The church does not belong to the elders, but the church is God's flock. An elder is a shepherd and a servant to take care of the owner's flock, and the owner is God Himself. In 1 Peter 5:3, Peter tells the elders not to lord it over the "allotments." This Greek word means lots or portions. The churches are God's possession, allotted to the elders as their allotments, their portions, entrusted to them by God for their care. God is the Owner and the Master and the elders are His servants to serve Him and take care of His assignment. The Master has assigned the local church to the elders who should take care of the flock, not by ruling but by serving as a slave, setting themselves up as living examples.

According to the New Testament teaching, there is no rank and no position for the elders. There is also no controlling for the elders because they do not have any rank or any position. They do not have any right to control. The clear word of the New Testament does not allow or give any ground for the elders to take rank, position, or controlling power.

## Spiritual Authority

Some who do not meet with us have already greatly misused Brother Nee's book *Spiritual Authority*. Brother Nee does not merely use the word authority, but his term is spiritual authority. Spiritual authority does not mean anything official, but something in life. When we say the elders have authority, we must not forget that the authority is not official. When anything becomes official, it is no longer something of life. Brother Nee does not talk of official authority but about spiritual authority. Since the authority is not official, there is no rank or position. Anything that is not official is not positional.

In the past, some young men came to us, taking the attitude that they were elders. They rebuked us, telling us that we did not know how to be elders. What they actually meant, however, was that we did not know how to control people. They knew how to control people based upon their misuse of *Spiritual Authority*. In my opinion, that book should be taken out of their hands.

If there is no rank, no position, and no controlling power for the elders, no one should be ambitious to be an elder. I do not believe anyone would be ambitious for slavery. It is not sufficient enough to tell people not to be ambitious. We must see that the holy Word takes away the rank, the position, and the controlling power of the elders; then no one would be ambitious.

Thus far, we have seen that in the New Testament there is no rank for the elders, and in this sense there is no position for the elders. Also, strictly speaking, there is even no authority given to the elders. First, the Lord Jesus charged us to be slaves, not to be masters or lords. A slave does not have any authority. Second, Peter, a fellow elder, charged the elders not to lord it over the flock but to be an example to take care of God's flock. We may ask, "Doesn't the shepherd have any authority over the flock?" God's flock, however, is not a flock of cattle. The shepherd who shepherds a flock of cattle does

not need to be an example. For a shepherd to be an example
to a flock of cattle is meaningless. Suppose that Peter charged
a real shepherd who shepherds a flock of sheep to be an
example to his flock. If this shepherd tried to tell his flock
that he received a charge from the Apostle Peter to be their
example, they would not understand what he was talking
about. We must see that the flock of God is not a flock of cattle
but of men, so the shepherd can, should, and must be an
example.

The word in Matthew 23 and in 1 Peter 5 does not give us
any hint that the elders have the authority. This shows us
that our understanding of the Bible is still greatly leavened.
We still have certain kinds of traditional, religious, human,
and natural understanding within us. To say that the elders
do not have any authority is against our natural thought.
However, if we would be quiet, and objective, and not hold on
to any kind of old understanding, allowing our mind to be
purified and sober, when we come to the pure Word, looking
to the Lord, we will see pure light.

## The Leading Ones

We should reexamine the Bible to see if any verse indicates or even hints that the elders have been assigned with
authority. Let us look at Hebrews 13:17: "Obey the ones leading you and submit to them, for they watch over your souls as
those who will give account, that they may do this with joy
and not groaning, for this would be unprofitable to you." We
may ask, "Doesn't the New Testament say in this verse that
the members in the church have to obey those who lead them?
Doesn't the word obey indicate that there is a certain kind of
authority?" This verse, however, tells us to obey the ones
leading us, not ruling us. We obey their leading, not their
authority. Merely by looking at the words obey and submit we
might understand that there is some authority with the
elders. But we must see that this verse does not tell us to
obey the rulers but to obey the leading ones.

When we were on mainland China we did not use the term
"leading ones." It was when we came to Taiwan that I began
to further consider this matter in the New Testament.

Hebrews 13:7 and 24 also refers to "the ones leading you." This corresponds with the thought of being an example. If you are going to be an example, you must take the lead. In order to help the saints get into the Word of God, you must do it first. You must take the lead. To obey the ones who lead means to obey their leading. The elders themselves should not claim any kind of obedience from the saints. They must check with themselves concerning how much leading they have rendered to the church, including the weak ones, the young ones, and the new ones. The actual situation, however, is that there has not been that much leading on the side of the elders, but there has been the claiming or requiring of the believers, the members, to be under them.

If we do not render the adequate leading, yet we claim, require, and demand obedience from the other members, this is a shame to us. For an elder not to render much leading to help the saints and yet to claim much obedience and submission from the saints is a shame, not a glory. How nice and how beautiful it would be to see that in the local churches there would only be the rendering of leading on the elders' side with no demand or no claim of the believers' obedience and submission.

Hebrews 13:17, of course, is a charge given to the members of the church. If the elders did not render any kind of leading or inadequately render the leading to the saints, then how could they claim that all the members should obey them? Hebrews 13:17 does not indicate the authority of the leading ones. It is not a matter of ruling, but a matter of leading. Strictly speaking in the New Testament, concerning the elders in the local churches, you cannot find a Greek word referring to the thought of ruling. If there were such a verse, it would contradict the Lord's word. The Lord's word is that among you there is no master, no ruler. Whoever wants to be great has to be a slave.

## THE FUNCTION OF THE ELDERS

### Managing the Church

Now we come to the function of the elders. According to 1 Timothy 3 and 5 we can see that the elders, first, have to manage the church just as a father manages his family, his house. First Timothy 3:4-5 says concerning the elders, "One who manages well his own household, having his children in subjection with all gravity; (But if anyone does not know how to manage his own household, how will he take care of the church of God?)." Some of us might be managers in a business. As a manager in a business we should not consider ourselves as a ruler. If a business manager considered himself as a ruler, he would be out of a position and no one would hire him. Even a father or a husband cannot take the attitude that he is ruling his family. If he conducts himself in this way, divorce from his wife and rebellion from his children will follow. Your ruling will rule out everybody and only rule in yourself. A father should not rule the family but manage it. In the same way, the church is our Father's home, His house, His family. He needs some human beings to manage His house for Him. For a father to manage a family is not simple. He has to acquire everything, and he has to prepare everything for the members of the family.

## Apt to Teach

First Timothy 3:2 tells us that an elder should be "apt to teach." The word apt implies being able and accustomed to. You may be very smart and have the ability to teach, but you may not have the habit of teaching and you may not like to teach because you are lazy. A mother cannot leave the family for half an hour, leaving the children alone without her. A mother cannot raise up children well in this way. The mother must be able to teach and must be apt to teach. She must have a teaching habit. If a local church has some elders who in their care of a local church are like mothers raising up their children, this would be wonderful. If a local church among us has elders teaching their members as a mother raising up her children, that church will be very good.

## Taking the Lead Well
## and Laboring in the Word and Teaching

First Timothy 5:17 shows us another aspect of the elder's function: "Let the elders who take the lead well be counted worthy of double honor, especially those who labor in word and teaching." This verse indicates that all the elders should be those who take the lead well. Therefore, these elders who take the lead well should receive double honor. Honor here means the life supply, which includes material supply for daily necessities. Because the elders are so occupied with the church, they do not have any time to make a living; therefore, the saints have to honor them by providing them with their daily necessities.

First Timothy also says that those who labor in word and teaching are especially worthy of double honor. All the elders have to take the lead. Among these elders who take the lead there may be some who have the burden to teach and to labor in the Word. These teaching ones are especially worthy of double honor. The reason for this is that nothing exhausts people more than teaching. Every good university professor and every good teacher in the elementary school is always occupied day and night. A teacher who is not occupied fully with his teaching could never be an adequate teacher. No other job occupies people like teaching. If I did not have to take care of the two annual trainings for teaching the Word, my life would be much easier. I would be able to sleep well without any burden. I could travel around the globe to hold meetings with little preparation. If you ask me, however, to be an elder in Anaheim, this is much harder.

The problems in a local church are mainly because of the lack of feeding. All the mothers know that to feed a family of eight people is not easy. The mother has to take care of the appetite and of the taste of the family. She must also cook the most nourishing foods. The mother's job is to feed the family even if they get bored with what she cooks and turn away. In like manner, we may present a message which the saints do not like. Then we have to pray and labor, finding a way to present the messages which the saints would desire to take and have an appetite for. Even if you are a genuine, typical mother, your children will run away after two weeks if they are not fed properly. Thus, you will lose your position as a mother. No one would take you as a mother. Your children need to be fed. They need something on which to live. It would be ridiculous for any mother to try to get her children on her side without taking care of the cooking. To feed a person with the best food is the way to win a person's heart.

Humanly speaking, if you want to keep your "position" you must feed the saints. Then your "position" will be fully secure. If you do not take this way, your position will not have a long life. If you take the political way of controlling the saints to win the saints over to you, you will lose your position.

## HAVING NO THOUGHT OF SECURING OUR POSITION

Never have any thought of securing your position. As long as I labor in the Word, render the teaching to the saints, and open up the Word to all the seeking ones, I do not need to secure my position. Some of the young ones among us may think that if they could not get a group of believers to work on, they would not have the security of their living. They may think, "If I don't have a church to work for, what shall I do? Then how could I make a living and be full-time?" I advise all of you, especially the young ones, to drop this thought. If you have this thought, I would advise you to go back to get a job to make a living. Do not go full-time with this kind of thought. When you go full-time, you must give your living "to the air." When I say this, I mean that you will never starve to death. The Lord will feed you and He has many ways to feed you. If you really mean business with Him, you do not need to take care of your position, and you do not need to think about your living. The Lord will give you your food.

This same fellowship applies to the elders. This is why I told the elders never to consider that the church is under their hand to maintain their position. Again I say that in the church, position is like the doves on the street. If you do not care for these doves, they may come to you. If you care for them and go after them, they will fly away. Position is just like this. If you like to get it, it flies away. If you do not care for it and care only for the Lord's interest, which includes the healthy condition of the church in which you are and the recovery of the Lord, your position is heavily secured. Otherwise, no matter what way you try to secure your position, it will not work. You will only damage yourself and damage others. This is why I felt the urgent need to have this training. Do not hold any work in your hand. Do not hold any church in your hand. Do not do anything to keep your position. This is altogether foolish.

## THE LORD'S WORK

As an older brother among you, I must testify that I have passed through all the roads already and that I know the roads. Most of you have not traveled on every road yet. I know what is not the right way. If you take the way I have warned you not to take, this will be a tragedy. I do not want to see this happen to you. We who are working for the Lord should not keep any work in our hand. This is not our work, but the Lord's work. We are just His slaves. The Lord tells us clearly in Luke that after doing our work, we have to come to our Master and say, "We are unprofitable slaves; we have done what we ought to have done" (17:10). Even if you have done much work, eventually you have to go to the Lord and say, "Lord, I am not useful. Forgive me." This should be our experience. No work is our work and no work should be in our hands.

## THE CHURCH—GOD'S POSSESSION

The elders also must realize that no church is their church. As we have seen, there are only three definitions used for the church—the church of God, the church of Christ, and the church of the saints. The church is not the church of the apostles nor of the elders. Rather, the elders are of the church. Do not consider the church you are now taking care of as your church. First Peter 5:2 indicates clearly that the church is God's possession assigned to your shepherding. The church is not your possession but God's possession. We are just little servants. All the elders are servants and all the churches are one Body bearing one testimony. Then we are under the blessing of the Lord. Otherwise, we miss the mark. When we miss the mark, we miss the blessing and then we have to struggle for ourselves. This is not the right way.

CHAPTER NINE

# PRACTICAL POINTS FOR THE ELDERS

### REPROVING A SINNING ELDER

In this chapter we will cover a number of crucial, practical points for the elders. First, we want to look at a charge which Paul gave to Timothy concerning his dealings with the elders in 1 Timothy 5:19-20: "Against an elder do not receive an accusation, except on the word of two or three witnesses. Those who sin reprove before all that the rest also may be in fear." In verse 20 there are three points—"those who sin" refers to elders, "all" refers to the whole church, and "the rest" refers to the other elders. Paul charged Timothy to reprove a sinning elder before the whole church. A sinning elder should receive public reproof because of his public position. The public reproof is so that the rest of the elders also may be in fear.

### NOT RULING BUT MANAGING

Thus far, we have seen from the Word that no rank is ascribed to the eldership and also, in a sense, no position. Of course, we have seen that even a small boy has a position in society, but in the sense of rank there is no position for the elders. Also, in a sense, no authority is ascribed to the elders based upon the Lord's word in Matthew 20:20-28 and Matthew 23:8-12. The Lord told us that among the believers there should be no master, no ruler. Whoever wants to be great has to serve as a slave. Basically speaking, no slave has any authority. Peter also told us that he was an elder, yet he told his fellow-elders not to lord it over God's possession, the flock, but to be an example.

In this sense we can see that the New Testament does not give authority for the elders to rule. When I mention the fact that no authority is given to the elders, I add the phrase "in a sense" because I have reserved something. The New Testament does not give the elders the authority in the sense of ruling, but there is still the sense of management. First Timothy indicates that the elders should manage God's house, No manager of a business is given the authority to rule the employees, but the manager surely has to manage the employees. In the sense of managing, we may consider that authority is given to the managing one.

Also, Hebrews 13:17 refers to the elders who take the lead in the church life. The saints are to obey the ones leading them. Even in the sense of leading the saints, there is some authority. In this sense, we can see that in a local church there is God's arrangement to keep a local church in a good order. In this sense, the elders have some authority, but we must be clear about this one thing—no authority has been given to the elders to rule over others. This is wrong. At the very most the elders are the managers of a house, not the ruler, the lord, or the master. We are told clearly in the New Testament that among the believers no one is a master and no one is a ruler. Peter also tells the elders not to lord it over the believers. The elders are not given any ruling authority.

## THE TEACHING OF IGNATIUS AND ITS ISSUE

Because of the wrong understanding of the New Testament, a system of bishops, the Episcopalian system, was established and this corrupted the entire church. Ignatius was negligent in his teaching of this matter. He understood that the word bishop, or overseer, refers to someone who is higher than an elder. The title of elders does not convey any denotation of ruling. An elder is a person of maturity. The word overseer, however, may be mistakenly understood to mean someone who is a controller. It was by this kind of overt understanding that Ignatius made a mistake which sowed the seed to produce the vast hierarchy in Christendom. Because of the history of Christianity which includes Catholicism with its great hierarchy of the pope, the cardinals, the archbishops, and the bishops, I have greatly stressed that no authority is given to the elders.

The papal system, in which the authority is ascribed to the pope, has ruined the church to the uttermost. In the hierarchy of the Catholic Church, there is actually no church and no Body of Christ, but just an organized, worldly system. In Catholicism the Body was killed and the church was annulled. Because of this, the Reformers reacted and many left the Catholic Church to form the Protestant churches. They came out of that worldly system, the Catholic Church, but they could not get away absolutely from the leaven which was brought in and that crept in secretly through Ignatius. Therefore, the beginning of the Protestant churches was the state churches. Among the state churches, the worst one in the matter of hierarchy is the Church of England which is very close to the Roman Catholic Church.

## THE MORAVIAN BROTHERS

Then there was a further move of the Lord through His lovers. Many believers began simply to adopt the title—the brothers or the brethren. Actually, this term was not firstly adopted by the British Brethren or the Plymouth Brethren. It was adopted even before the time of Zinzendorf, mostly in northern Europe. When the Moravian brothers came to Zinzendorf, they began to have a church life outside of Catholicism and absolutely outside of the organized Protestant churches. At that time, the Moravian brothers and many others suffered persecution from two sources—the Catholic Church and the state churches. These brothers were compelled to go to Bohemia to Zinzendorf. He took the lead to establish a very good church life. Although the church life in Bohemia was not fully according to the Bible, it was still very much according to the Bible.

## THE BRETHREN

Approximately one century later, the Brethren in England were raised up. They came out of the organization of both the Catholic and Protestant churches to the uttermost. They dropped everything of hierarchy and denominationalism.

This was a very strong reaction to the papal system, the Episcopalian system, and the Protestant system. They stressed the Body very much. They saw very little, however, of the principle of the resurrection life for the Body. At least they did not see what we see today concerning this matter. They did see, though, that the church was the Body of Christ and they stressed the Body greatly.

## SPIRITUAL AUTHORITY

Later, seeking Christians were raised up who concentrated on the inner life. They also reacted to the papal system and to the Protestant organization. As a result, a "loose" condition was produced among the believers. Some of the seeking Christians began to oppose any kind of authority. They did not regard or respect anyone. Due to the rise of democratic forms of government, another factor which invaded the Christian concept was that the church should be democratic.

Brother T. Austin-Sparks began to see that most Christians neglected the matter of spiritual authority. His understanding was based upon the spiritual authority in the Body of Christ. For example, in our physical body there is the authority in life. All the members obey the headship, the authority of the head. The head directs all the members of the body. Beginning with Brother Sparks, the stress on spiritual authority came out. Brother Nee saw the same thing. Therefore, Brother Nee wrote the book *Spiritual Authority*. I never read this book, because actually, before Brother Nee wrote the book, he talked to me personally about this matter. He told me its entire contents.

If we receive any teaching carelessly, this can always cause some subsidiary mistake. Many outsiders use Brother Nee's teaching on spiritual authority as their ground to exercise, not their spiritual authority, but their human authority. They do not exercise the authority in life but the authority by organization. There has also been a by-product among us of such a subsidiary mistake. This by-product is the thought that a certain brother is the first among the co-workers or that another brother is the first among the elders.

## IN LIFE

We should practice the church life according to the instruction of the New Testament, not in a legal way, but in the way of life with love. We must realize that the church life can only be practiced rightly in life with love. Any instruction given by the New Testament concerning the church life should be kept in life. If you are out of life, you are through with the church life. The church is not a matter of organization or regulation but altogether a matter of the resurrection life.

Life in the New Testament and especially in the Epistles means the resurrection life, which is the resurrected Christ as the life-giving Spirit. The church must be practiced by our being in this life. Many Christians are missing the mark because they do not care for this life. They care for the Bible doctrines and instructions in letters. They study the Bible instructions and teachings concerning their religion just like the lawyers studying law. We should not take the Word of God, however, merely according to the black and white letters of the Bible. We have to get into its spirit, and the spirit of the New Testament is the resurrected Christ as life to us. The constitution of the church life is not a number of regulations like the constitution of the United States. The constitution of the church life is of the life element. It is of life, it is a matter of life, and its element must be life. When we practice the church, we must practice it in the resurrection life.

## IN LOVE

Also, we must realize that the small phrase "in love" is used six times in the book of Ephesians (1:4; 3:17; 4:2, 15, 16; 5:2). We may pick up the things mentioned in Ephesians, yet neglect this little phrase—in love. In Ephesians five Paul charges the wives to submit themselves to their husbands (v. 22). Paul does not say, however, that the wives submit and that the husbands rule. Paul says that the wives submit and the husbands love (v. 25). A husband should not rule but love. If a husband firstly rules, he will eventually eat the fruit of separation and lastly he will eat the final fruit—divorce. Ruling only brings forth separation and then divorce. The best way for a husband to have the best wife is to love her to the uttermost. The more you love her, the better she becomes. The worst wife can be the best by the husband's loving.

Submission is on the wife's side. On the husband's side there should not be ruling but loving. In like manner, submission is on the believers' side, but on the elders' side there should not be ruling but loving. When the elders try to rule, the issue will be "separation and divorce." If the elders are ruling the saints in their locality, they will eat the fruit of this in the future. The elders must learn how to love. The more they love the better. In the family life, in the church life, and in the neighborhood life to love is best. We must learn this lesson—to love.

Managing and leading gives the elders some kind of authority to say something. They must remember, however, not to say or do anything without love. Let love protect you. Let love balance you. In your leadership, always do something in love. In your management always say and do things in love. This is the best. This will protect the church, this will preserve the saints, and this will preserve you.

### NO SPECIAL GROUP

Also, the elders should not let any kind of special group come into existence in the church. First, as a leading one in the local church, you should not practice to attract a small number of saints to be your people, your group. Once you do this, you will open the door for some other groups to arise. We human beings are very prone and apt to do this. Because I am one of the leaders and I need someone to help me, this could become a cloak under which I build up a small group. Actually, that small group becomes not only your helper, but also your "spies" to collect information for you to protect your interests. Many years ago in China, I saw a locality in which five elders had formed two groups. This happens in any kind of society or in any kind of human organization, but this should be altogether put aside in the church life. Do not take any lead to form a group. This will corrupt the church. Whenever such a thing is produced in your church, immediately there are spies on every side. The persons in a certain group are always collecting information. While they are doing this, others who are not in any group would also collect information. As a result, in most of the church meetings, the main job might be to collect information.

We all love the Lord, we all love the church, and we all love the recovery. This is why we are in the recovery, but we human beings have our weakness in our fallen nature. We like to know others' things and we like to keep all things secret. Also, we like to protect our own interests. As a result, there is a basic element of competition compelling us to get helpers, especially when a brother becomes an elder. Before he became an elder, he was nobody. Then after he became an elder, he considered himself to be somebody. Spontaneously, then, a group is formed and sometimes this group which was formed was due to a very positive need. You may need some helpers in your work, but when you get the help you must try to stay away from forming a close group. Once you do this, you damage yourself. You get the benefit and the help temporarily, but that help contains many corrupting germs.

By the Lord's mercy I have always had very close helpers, but I do not have any close group. I have stayed in the United States, working and living here for over twenty-two years. None of the brothers, however, can say that they are very close to Brother Lee. Whoever has said this has left the recovery. I do not have any close ones. All the brothers are one with me "at a distance." The only one you should be close to without distance is your wife. If you are close to anyone without any distance besides your wife, this is corruption. God has ordained that only a couple, husband and wife, should be absolutely one, even one flesh without any distance. With a man and a wife there is not only no distance but also no separation. A man and wife are one flesh. However, we should not be one with anyone, other than our wife, without some distance.

Keeping a distance in this way preserves you and keeps the Lord's work from being corrupted. This also keeps the church from being ruined and keeps your helpers very healthy in the Spirit. We all have to pray, "Lord, have mercy upon us that in the local church where we are there would not be a spy." I am not referring to opposers, but to so-called parties in the local church as spies. I must regretfully say that in some localities some spying goes on even at the Lord's table. This has to be killed. Whenever someone comes to you to talk in this way you should not talk and you should stop his talk. This is why gossiping in the church life always brings the death element everywhere and to everyone.

We must also realize that the sisters, with their female nature, are very subjective and cannot be objective as easily as the brothers can. We must also realize that subjectivity always opens the door for corruption to come in. The brothers do not fall into friendships so easily, but the sisters do. Unintentionally, some of the sisters may spontaneously form a group. If you would tell some of the sisters not to form this kind of group around themselves they would say, "Praise the Lord. I don't have one." Actually they have one unintentionally. Immediately after this kind of speaking, one sister may go to another and tell her, "The brothers indicated that we sisters easily form groups among ourselves. I don't have one, do you?" The sister might respond that they do not have a group. Actually, however, these two sisters are one group already. Immediately after the brothers' speaking, this sister would always go to certain other sisters and never to some other ones. Eventually, these two sisters and the other ones in their group begin to tell one another how terrible it is that the brothers are always belittling the sisters. They may even have a "telephone conference" which is eventually filled with negative talk and gossip. This is a corruption and a ruin. By the Lord's mercy always try to avoid this and to kill it. This does not mean that you have to "declare war" on the sisters involved in this. As elders who take the lead to shepherd the church, to feed the flock, we should always minister life. If we hold such an attitude of exercising our spirit to minister life to the flock, life itself will kill the germs.

### DEALING WITH A SINNING ONE

When the elders who are taking care of the church deal with some sinning ones, they should not condemn his family. If this sinning one is a brother, we should only deal with him.

Do not consider his entire family as victims. Rather, when we deal with a sinning brother, we must love his wife and love his children. If this brother would not repent after a long, long period of patience on the elders' side and if he would not give up his sinning life, this would force the church to remove him. Do not include his wife or his children in your dealing. Rather, you must love the wife and the children even more. It is not so easy or simple to take care of the church.

## NOT TRUSTING IN MAN BUT IN THE LORD

Do not think that you should be able to fully trust in your helpers. When the Lord Jesus selected the twelve, He selected Judas. I believe that one of the lessons indicated by the Lord here is that we should not hope to have helpers in whom we can fully trust. We always have to put our trust in the Lord (Jer. 17:5, 7). Romans three also indicates that no one is trustworthy and that only God is true and faithful (v. 4). Only God is faithful because all of us human beings are weak and selfish. You may trust me very much, and your trusting in me always makes me happy. However, you cannot make me happy all the time. Something will eventually happen that will make me unhappy with you. Once this happens, that might become a factor in me. This little factor could grow and grow and eventually the unhappiness will increase.

This shows us that we should not trust in man, but trust in the Lord. This will avoid a lot of damaging issues. This will not only protect you, but also protect the one in whom you trust. Even though we have all been regenerated and a number among us have been greatly transformed, we are still human and still in the old creation. We all have our weak points. I would not want any of you to trust in me fully. I am not that perfect, able, or capable. If you trust in me fully and completely with no reservation, you will delay yourself. Also, you will destroy me, you will destroy yourself, and you will destroy the entire situation. You have to consider that I am merely a man. I might be a little more capable than you are, but I am not almighty. I may be a good brother, but I am not absolutely perfect.

Therefore, we all must exercise some kind of caution and some kind of discernment. We should love each other and we should trust in each other, yet we have to realize that we are all still human. Overtrusting really damages. Not to trust is wrong, but to trust in full is also wrong. Not trusting in full does not mean that you do not trust. In the church life we should always have caution and consideration, but this does not give you the ground to be suspicious. There are always two sides to everything.

### MARRIAGE

We must always keep in mind that the real, actual, and prevailing function of the elders is to minister life, to feed people. Based upon this principle, I would like to pass on a very crucial and practical point to you. The elders should stay away from the saints' practical life matters such as marriage. The saints may come to you, especially the young ones, to get your help concerning their marriage, their choice in marriage, and even concerning their dating. I do not mean that we older ones should not help them, but there is a great temptation in helping them in these kinds of things. Eventually, we could fall into directing them or even somewhat controlling them. This is very dangerous.

When young saints came to me forty-five years ago, I always had some principles and regulations to pass on to them. I always had the instructions ready, and I fully trusted that my principles were really right and prevailing. After a period of time, I learned not to do this. Today if anyone comes to me to talk about their marriage or about their choice in marriage, I have no burden and no interest. I have learned not to give the young saints advice concerning whom they will marry. I even told my closest relatives to just trust in the Lord concerning their marriage. Only the Lord knows who is a good match for another person. We do not know.

I saw many cases of wonderful brothers who all became "ugly" in their marriage. Also, some nice sisters became different persons immediately after their wedding. There have been a number of cases like this in the history of the church life. About fifty years ago, we had a marvelous, promising, young group of medical students in China. Nearly all these medical students were saved. A good number of them met with us in the church. We expected great things from them, but after their weddings most of them gradually became cold and did not go on in the Lord's recovery quite well. This was mostly due to their marriage. Therefore, in the church life all we can do concerning the young people's marriage is to minister life to them. We must help them to look to the Lord's leading, to learn how to walk in the Spirit, and we should also help them not to indulge in lust or to have their own taste or choice. This is all we can do. We should not try to conduct them into a marriage or match them.

To invite a brother and sister together to dinner for the purpose of bringing them together should be done with adequate consideration. Do not do this in a loose or subjective way. There should not be any kind of controlling among us concerning the young saints' marriage. I do not believe that there is anyone controlling, but there is a temptation that the older ones among us would think that they could help the young ones. This, however, is the human hand, not the Lord's hand. We should not touch this matter. For example, a white shirt may be very clean but after this shirt is touched by us for five days it becomes dirty just because of our touching. Our hands are not absolutely clean.

The matter of marriage is very complicated and is most perplexing. We should try to be very objective and try to render life to the young ones. Never try to bring two people together without any caution. This is dangerous. Some of you may feel that you did this once and that you were very successful. You may have been successful in one marriage, but do not take that as an encouragement. There is no need for us to touch this matter in a natural way. We should leave this matter to the Lord and pray for the ones concerned. We should render as much life as we can to help them and never indicate who is their best match. We do not control, and even the more, we do not conduct or indicate what brother or sister might be best for them. If we leave this matter to the Lord, we will save the church much trouble. The more the leading ones touch people's marriage, the more they get involved.

This indicates that the church is sick in a certain point. Even in helping the saints in their jobs, we must be careful. I do not mean that we should not help the saints in these kinds of matters; we should help the saints in every way, but we must be careful.

On the other hand, when the elders realize that some young saints are dating in an improper way, they must render them some help. They should tell the ones concerned that it is altogether not safe for a young brother to be with a young sister in a loose way. Also, the elders should help them to consider their future. They should consider the matter of not getting engaged too quickly before marriage. They also must consider things regarding their family, their parents, their job, their financial situation, and other responsibilities. This is a real help in their human life. Sometimes young people are careless and are too much in their lust. We should help them to learn how to pray about their marriage and how to look to the Lord to restrict their indulgence and lust. We have to help them in morality, in human life, in spirituality, and in the Lord's way. They are young in the Lord and need this kind of help. On the one hand, we should not interfere with them; on the other hand, we have to help them in morality, in life, in human living, in taking care of the future, concerning their parents, and even in praying and seeking the Lord concerning the one whom they marry not being their choice. They should be helped to leave this matter to the Lord. As elders, we should do this because we are shepherding the flock. However, we should not touch their marriage and we should not think that we have the ability to match them. To help the saints in the matter of their weddings is a "pure help." There is nothing wrong with this. To help them sign the papers for their marriage does not mean that we are doing our best to bring them together. The Lord has already brought them together.

## MONEY

Now we come to the matter of finance, of money. It is not easy to create a financial condition which is profitable to the saints. It is always good not to bring the saints together in the matter of money. Money is a hard thing to handle. Do not think that just because we are brothers in the church life who love one another that it is all right for us to do business with one another. As an older brother among you, I would advise you not to have financial relationships with brothers. Do not get into a partnership with brothers and even the more with sisters. I want to warn you based upon my own experiences in the past.

If you help a brother get a loan from another brother, you must prepare yourself to pay that loan. If you are not prepared to pay that loan, keep your hands off. It is better to be spiritual. Tell the brother who wants the loan that you will pray for him. This brother may feel strongly that you can help him in this matter. Again I say, however, do not touch the matter of marriage and do not touch the matter of money. We should help the saints in a very profitable way, but with certain practical limitations. Even if we recommend a certain brother for a job, we must do it carefully. These are problems in human society.

We are regenerated and we love the Lord, but practical things still cause trouble. The biggest troubles in human society are sex, money, and business. If these three items were removed from human society, every country would be full of peace. None of the elders should touch these three things. Do not touch the matters of marriage, money, and business without caution. We must love our brothers. If we have the ability to help a certain brother, then we can give to him. Some of the churches have suffered in these matters already, but thank the Lord, not that much. The longer a church exists in a certain place, the greater the possibility there is that there would be involvement in these three matters. These matters can all become temptations to the elders.

### IN TRUTH, IN LIFE, AND IN LOVE

As a leading one in the church, you should always move, act, and practice in truth, in life, and in love. This will be quite healthy. We must stay in these three things. We must realize that there are germs everywhere. Our physical body can easily get sick. Even while the fruits and vegetables are growing on the farm, the farmers try to find a way to protect the fruits and the vegetables from being corrupted or contaminated. In the church life it is the same way. The entire human society is thoroughly sick. There are germs everywhere. If we are careless and do not stand strictly in the truth, in life, and in love, it will be hard for us not to be contaminated. This is why we should pray much and always be careful and trembling in contacting the brothers and in helping them. Always learn to be fearful and trembling and to do things in truth, in life, and in love. Then you will be protected. This does not mean that we will not have any problems. Even a very healthy person can get sick with just a little carelessness. In order to keep ourselves healthy, we must be very careful all day. With just a little carelessness, we will get sick. All of us love the Lord, love His recovery, love the church life, and love all the saints, but do not think that merely to have a loving heart is sufficient. We must stick ourselves to truth, keep ourselves in love, and always help others in life. This is safe.

CHAPTER TEN

# THE CHINESE-SPEAKING WORK

## THE IMMIGRATION FACTOR

Since 1983 we have felt led of the Lord to take care of the Chinese-speaking work in the United States and in Canada. When I first came to the United States, I had a clear feeling that I should not spend much time with the Chinese-speaking work in order to concentrate the work for the recovery among the English-speaking saints. We all have seen that this work was very much under the Lord's blessing. In 1967, though, the United States immigration law was renewed, giving a quota of twenty thousand immigrants to the Chinese people yearly. This means that from 1967 until today, twenty thousand Chinese people have come to the United States every year. By 1982, approximately three hundred thousand Chinese people had come to the United States. Beginning in 1982, the United States government added another twenty thousand to the quota of Chinese immigrants. This was mainly due to the United States' relationship with Red China. Therefore, from 1982 forty thousand Chinese immigrants have been coming to the United States every year.

Some of these Chinese immigrants are students who are studying to attain a high degree. Many of these immigrants already have their master's degree or their Ph.D. and they all have a high rank in their jobs. Other immigrants include the direct relatives of these college graduates such as parents, wives, brothers, or sisters. Still other immigrants are rich people who could afford to make some investment in the United States. I have considered that this situation is an answer of the Lord to the prayers of so many dear saints, including those good missionaries who went to China. Their prayers for the great race of China are now being answered. China was closed to the gospel for many, many years. So much prayer has been offered to the Lord by His faithful saints that today on this earth, the Chinese are easy to bring to the Lord. This is especially true in the educational circles—the universities, including the graduate schools. This is true not only in one country, but everywhere on this earth. Even the rich Chinese people are easy to bring to the Lord.

I have been observing the situation among the Chinese-speaking people since I came to the United States. Immediately after the new immigration law was put into force in 1967, I noticed something among the Chinese-speaking citizens or residents in this country. However, I still did not have a clear view that I would be spending some time to take care of this part of the work. Then in 1980 a Chinese-speaking meeting was begun in Anaheim. In 1983 I began to feel led of the Lord that we should not miss the chance to work on these Chinese students on their campuses and also on the Chinese community. At the present time in the United States, there are approximately one and a half million Chinese people. In California the total number of Chinese immigrants is approximately three hundred thousand, which is one-fifth of the total Chinese population in this country. Approximately one hundred and fifty thousand of these immigrants live around Los Angeles. Also, a large number of these have settled in the Orange County, California area. This is why there are many "Chinese churches" in the Southern California area.

## OUR COOPERATION IN THE WORK

Throughout the years, we have not done much work among the Chinese-speaking people. Due to this, we have lost a number of them. Among these Chinese immigrants over the years, a good number were saints who were among us in Taiwan and in Hong Kong. When they came to this country, they got scattered. Because we did not do much to take care of them, they were lost. All the young ones among them, who were studying in the schools, became very prevailing factors

among the scattered Chinese Christian groups. We must realize that nearly everywhere in the United States on the
campuses there are Chinese students and Chinese Christian
fellowships which are in the Chinese language. Wherever
there are a number of Chinese on a certain campus, there is a
Chinese Christian fellowship. In these fellowships many of
the speaking ones and leading ones are products of the
churches in Taiwan and of the church in Hong Kong. This
means they went out from us. A few of these are dissenting,
but most of them are still for the Lord's recovery.

This situation led us to reconsider our attitude. Beginning in 1983, we felt that we could not go on any further
without paying adequate attention to this part of the work.
Otherwise, we would suffer much. Within the past year, we
have had two Chinese-speaking conferences with about
eleven hundred attendants for the first conference and
twelve hundred to thirteen hundred attendants for the
second conference. Within one year's time, from 1983 to
1984, twenty-nine Chinese-speaking meetings have
been raised up in the local churches. The number of people
in these Chinese-speaking meetings is also increasing. A
number of the churches can testify how the Lord has blessed
this and how this has become a help to the church in their
locality.

I feel that our cooperation with the Lord in this work is
very crucial. Of course, this is not a direct work with the
English-speaking people. However, I believe that since most
of the young generation of these Chinese immigrants are
graduates with master's degrees and Ph.D. degrees, when
they get saved, gained by the Lord, and trained with the New
Testament economy, the truth of the recovery will be chan-
neled through them to the English-speaking people. The
present situation among us is that the Chinese-speaking
people, the community at large and the students, are very
open to the gospel. Also, a number of Chinese Christian fellowships use our materials and have our books. We have
to follow the Lord's sovereign arrangement. This situation is
something sovereign of the Lord. This does not mean, however, that we are going to establish Chinese churches. This

means that we are establishing the local churches with all races.

## THE LANGUAGE PROBLEM

We need the Chinese-speaking meeting because a number of the immigrants who are the relatives and the parents of the young graduates do not know much English. They may be able to speak enough English to get by in their business, but they have a real problem listening to a message in a Christian meeting. They also have a hard time listening to the testimonies and they cannot praise or pray, uttering their feelings to the Lord freely. Because of this situation, these Chinese Christians have suffered greatly. As a result, they went somewhere else to a Chinese meeting. Some of their children are coming to our meetings, but they will not come because they cannot understand anything. They are forced to go to other's Chinese Christian meetings. This shows us that there is the need of meeting the problem of this language barrier.

In addition to this, even the younger generation who graduated from the schools in the United States still have a problem with the language. They also can function with the English language adequately in their business or in their school, but it is difficult for them to listen to a message. It is also difficult for them to utter something in prayer or in praise. Because they feel awkward, this becomes a frustration to them. Once a Chinese-speaking meeting begins, they immediately become happy and released. Even the ones who graduated from the universities in the United States are really happy and feel released. They can utter everything in their prayer, praise, and testimonies. Some of the English-speaking saints who have come to the Chinese-speaking conferences and who have had to use the earphones for translation, have learned to sympathize with the Chinese. They know what a suffering it is to wear the earphones and now they understand more of the problem. These English-speaking saints testified that they are now qualified to sympathize with so many Chinese who must wear the earphones in the meeting for translation. This is really a suffering. Again, we can see that the need is here.

## CHINESE-SPEAKING MEETINGS
## NOT CHINESE CHURCHES

We must realize that we are not setting up Chinese churches. These Chinese-speaking meetings are a part of the local church and these meetings are still under the one eldership. This is absolutely a part of the local church and not an independent church. In some places the saints may feel awkward concerning this. They may feel that this would begin to make the church in their locality Chinese. Also, some of the saints may not be happy to see that in one building a Chinese-speaking Lord's table is going on upstairs and an English-speaking Lord's table is going on downstairs. They may not understand how one church can have two kinds of Lord's tables at one time. This may become a bothering to certain saints.

The elders should do their best to make this situation understandable to the saints. This is entirely for the Lord's interest. All the churches can testify that the Chinese-speaking saints have really been a strengthening to the local churches. The Chinese-speaking meeting has always been a positive thing and a strengthening to the church. This is not only a help to the Chinese-speaking side of the church but also an indirect help to the English-speaking side of the church. This is a plus to the church in the increase, in the financial support, and in the functioning of all the members. This has been and still is a real help to the Lord's recovery. Perhaps it would be better to have a joint Lord's table once a month in a locality for the English-speaking saints and for the Chinese-speaking saints. Thus, at least once a month all would come together in order to keep a "mingled" atmosphere. This may also be quite profitable.

When we use the term "Chinese-speaking meeting," we stress the word speaking. We do not consider that it is a Chinese meeting, which is based upon the race. This meeting is based upon the language. We have made it clear that anyone who can manage the English language for the purpose of the meeting must go to the English-speaking meeting. The Chinese-speaking meeting does not depend upon race but upon your language. If anyone can manage the Chinese language, he is free to come to the Chinese-speaking meeting.

## THE CAMPUS WORK

We are hoping that the Lord can raise up a number of young people who are bilingual to go full-time. These ones would be useful to go and visit all of the campuses. Also, if the Lord wills, we will have summer conferences and training centers. The full-time ones could go to visit the campuses to work on the "farms." When summer comes, the school terms will be over. Then all these ones who are reaped will probably be able to give two weeks to attend a conference plus a training concerning the Christian life. These would then go back to the campuses as seeds which are sown to grow into another harvest. We also hope that we could have a long period of training of maybe two or three months to train the ones who are willing to bear some responsibility in the Chinese-speaking work and in the Chinese-speaking meetings. Also, all the full-timers need this kind of training.

Because of this situation, we felt that it might be very profitable to have some houses close to the major campuses. We could call a certain house near a campus "the Chinese student center." We do not need to use the word Christian in referring to the student center because we accept the unbelievers. This kind of Chinese student center would help the new ones coming from Hong Kong and mostly from Taiwan. They are new in the United States and they do not know where to go or what to do practically. With such a center near a campus, we will have some way to help them and to lodge them. Spontaneously, the host of this house would be able to render some help to them in the gospel. This will give the Lord a way to reap many. I feel that this is a golden time for us to go on with the Lord in this matter. Then we could do something for His move today on this earth. This work will also exercise a great effect on the English-speaking community. We all need to pray for this.

## THE LORD'S SOVEREIGNTY

The Lord is really sovereign in the world situation. Due to the political change in mainland China, a number of Chinese fled to Taiwan and we were among them. The Lord did a marvelous work on that island. Within ten years the Lord gained about fifty thousand. The reason why we could have over one thousand Chinese-speaking saints in a conference is because of this source of Taiwan. The fact that the number of Chinese immigrants to the United States has been increased from twenty-thousand to forty-thousand is another factor for the Lord's move. This is all sovereign of the Lord. Many Chinese come yearly to the United States and among these are many of the dear saints. The Lord has sovereignly prepared these ones for coming to the United States. I believe that one by one they all will become a strengthening to the Lord's recovery in the United States. Again, this is something really sovereign of the Lord.

## THE RECOVERY OF THE LOST ONES

Among the Chinese immigrants who are living in the United States, quite a few thousand came from the source of the local churches. Among these, only about two thousand are now in the local churches in the United States and Canada. We are hoping that through this Chinese-speaking work, many of them will be brought back to the Lord's recovery. Some have already come back within this past year. This is also something for which we need to pray.

# CHAPTER ELEVEN

## OUR ATTITUDE
## TOWARD FELLOW-BELIEVERS

### OUR VISION

The Lord has really opened up His Word to us since 1920 mainly through Brother Watchman Nee. According to what the Lord has shown us through His holy Word, I would say that the Lord's testimony in the New Testament age is Christ as the all-inclusive One. He is not only the embodiment of the Triune God (Col. 2:9), but also a Man as the Head of the old creation (Eph. 1:22; Col. 1:15b). As the One who accomplished redemption for our salvation, He is the Redeemer (John 1:29; 1 Pet. 1:18-19), and He is also the Savior (Luke 2:11; John 4:42). Through His death in the flesh and resurrection in the Spirit, He became the life-giving Spirit (1 Cor. 15:45b). In resurrection He became the Head of God's new creation. He was the Head of the old creation of God. As the resurrected Christ, He has produced the church and has become the Head of the church as His Body (Col. 1:18). He is now on the throne, crowned and enthroned as the Christ and the Lord of all (Acts 2:36; 10:36). He is coming back as the Bridegroom to the church (John 3:29; Rev. 19:7), as the Judge to the world (2 Tim. 4:1), and as the very Savior to God's chosen people, Israel (Rom. 11:26). Then He will be the King of the entire universe in the millennium (Rev. 20:6; 19:16). By this we can see that Christ is all-inclusive.

God's intention is to work this Christ into His chosen people (Gal. 1:16a; 2:20a; 4:19) to make them His new creation (2 Cor. 5:17; Gal. 6:15) and give them the divine sonship (Eph. 1:5; Gal. 3:26), making them regenerated (John 3:6) and transformed (2 Cor. 3:18) members of Christ's Body (1 Cor. 12:27). This Body is the church in this age (Eph. 1:22-23a) and on this earth to be expressed in cities as local churches (Rev. 1:11) without organization and without the nature of the old creation. The resurrected Christ is its constitution (Col. 3:11; 1 Cor. 12:12). This is what the Lord has shown us throughout the past years.

## A GREAT DISCREPANCY

By His mercy, the Lord opened our eyes to see such a vision. When we compared Christendom with what we had seen of the Lord's vision we saw a great discrepancy, a great difference. We saw three categories of things which were altogether not scriptural and not according to the vision that the Lord had shown us from His holy Word.

## Division

The first discrepancy we saw was the matter of division. What the Lord had shown us in this vision from His holy Word was one unique people chosen by the one unique God and saved, regenerated, to be the one unique Body of Christ as the unique church of God. When we looked at Christendom, however, we saw division after division in nearly every city. Sometimes we even saw divisions on the same streets. One certain street became a so-called church market. This shocked us when we compared what we had seen with the actual situation. We were young people who were purely seeking the Lord Himself according to His holy Scriptures and this shocked us.

## Organization

Based upon this, we also saw another matter in Christendom which we could not find in the Bible—organization. In the Bible there is no human organization. As the chosen people of God, we all have been reborn of God to have His divine sonship. Then we become the organic Body of Christ. The Body is organic and is altogether an organism not an organization. How could the organic Body be something organized? We were bothered when we compared this to the revelation that we had seen. The organizations of

Christianity were the second category of things which we surely could not agree with according to the vision we had received.

## Traditions

A third item that did not match the vision we have seen from the Scriptures was the matter of traditions. By the Lord's mercy the Lord caught us when we were students. We loved the Lord, and we loved the Bible. We dove into the Bible, and within a few years, the Lord gave us a clear vision. Then when we turned to look at Christianity, we saw divisions, organizations, and traditions. We heard a little concerning the name of Jesus Christ the Son of God, and we heard a little of the shallow gospel. We hardly heard any truth, but we saw many traditions. This was the reason the Lord did something to raise us up that we might stand up to begin something outside the divisions and without organization and unscriptural traditions.

### PRACTICING TO BEAR GOD'S TESTIMONY AS THE RETURNED REMNANT

We then began to meet so purely and so bravely according to the Bible. This was the start. We did not know much, but we saw divisions, organizations, and traditions in Christianity, which we could not follow according to the pure Word of God. We loved the Lord, and we loved His Word. We wanted to give our life to Him. Our first love was the Lord and His truth. This was our beginning. Then the Lord brought us into contact with some top missionaries. Through them we were brought into the Christian books, including the classical books, church history, and biographies from the second century until that time. All these writings further confirmed us.

From the very beginning we realized that despite the divisions, organizations, and traditions, there were a great number of genuine Christians scattered in these divisions. We saw that the Lord's Body comprises all these genuine believers. Even in the Catholic Church we saw a number of genuine believers, and we also considered them as members of the church and as our dear brothers and sisters. On the one hand, we began to meet by ourselves and we fully realized that the dear, genuine believers who were scattered in the Catholic Church and the Protestant denominations were our brothers. We recognized them and we loved them. We realized that the Lord's Body as the church of God did not only comprise us but also all the genuine believers, of which we were a small part. On the other hand, we also realized that they were not remaining in the proper church life. At the beginning, we did not see the genuine ground of the church, but we still realized that many of our dear brothers did not remain in the proper church life. They had been scattered into divisions in their organizations with all the traditions.

At this juncture, the Lord showed us the type in the Old Testament of the children of Israel being scattered to Syria, to Egypt, and to Babylon. When God came in to call them back to His chosen land, very few responded. The majority remained in their captivity. We realized from the Old Testament that these ones who were turned to build up the destroyed temple were the remnant of God's people. The majority of the children of Israel remained in the heathen land, but only a small number, a remnant, came back to God's chosen land.

We understood this type and we considered ourselves as the fulfillment of that type. We were the remnant of God's people who had come back to His original intention while so many genuine believers had been scattered and still remained in their captivity. We love our brothers and desire that they would come this way. In the same way, in the Old Testament the returned remnant loved those who still remained in their captivity. They expected that many who were in captivity would come back to join them for God's testimony. These returned ones immediately began to build the temple. The size of this temple was not as great as the original one, yet in principle it was the same and was considered as God's testimony. God honored what they did because He was with them and His glory was there.

This vision and understanding strengthened our faith. We believed that, even though we were very small, we were the recovered testimony of God. This testimony is God's dwelling place filled with His glory. We had the assurance that God's glory was with us. I hope we can see that even by that time we brothers were clear concerning our attitude toward the Christians who did not meet with us. We realized that all of them were members of the Body of Christ. We loved them, yet they were scattered and still remained in their captivity. We not only loved them but also expected that they would come to join us to bear God's testimony.

This is the second point of our attitude toward other Christians. The first point is that we have seen God's vision and by God's vision we realized the real condition of today's Christendom. Based upon this vision, we practiced bearing God's testimony as the returned remnant.

Undoubtedly, God had given His truths to us. In expounding any verse, we would go back directly to the Greek text. We did not study Greek, yet we had dictionaries, lexicons, and concordances to help us in our study. Brother Nee took the lead to say that since the Lord had given us the truths in this age, we must go out and send this truth to the denominations. I was the one who probably did this work the most. I was sent out to travel from province to province and to city after city in North China. Wherever I went I was warmly welcomed because I presented the truth which they mostly had never heard before. The result I saw, however, was not encouraging. This was like bringing the water out of a deep well and pouring it upon the earth. The earth became wet for maybe one day, and then the next day all the water went back to the same place from where it was brought up.

Due to the Japanese invasion of China, many of us were scattered, and I realized that that work was not so profitable to the Lord's recovery. Therefore, I changed my concept and I did not go out but stayed in my home town of Chefoo for approximately five years, from 1938 through 1943. This issued in a revival breaking out in Chefoo. Through all these experiences, we have learned much. Due to the political situation after the war, I could not stay in the north, so the brothers asked me to go to the south to stay with them in Nanking and in Shanghai. In Shanghai I met Brother Nee again and presented all that I had experienced and had seen to him, including the things concerning the practical church life. He absolutely confirmed the things I fellowshipped with him.

Because of such a successful practice of the church life in Chefoo and in Shanghai, I was fully occupied. I was in Shanghai less than two and a half years from the end of 1946 to the beginning of 1949. I mainly stayed in Shanghai and spent part of my time in Nanking. I was so occupied that I did not have any time to do any other work. I did not have the time to have any more contact with other Christians who did not meet with us. I was fully occupied with the preaching of the gospel, the teaching of the Bible, the edifying of the saints, and the building up of the church. In those two and a half years I was absolutely in the eldership even though I was not an elder. Even though I did not do everything myself, I also took care of the business affairs. I was fully occupied.

Then the political situation changed and that forced us to leave mainland China and go to Taiwan. When we arrived in Taiwan, we began a work which was very much blessed by the Lord, so, again I was more than occupied. Quite often I also went to the Philippines from Taiwan. I spent approximately two-thirds of my time in Taiwan and the rest of my time in the Philippines. From 1950 I began to publish the Chinese magazine—*The Ministry of the Word*. This magazine has continued to be published up to the present time. In those early days, I myself composed the articles or rewrote the messages I gave to place in this magazine. I also received a little help from the brothers to write some articles on church history and some gospel messages. This shows again that I was fully occupied.

This does not mean that I had no intention of going out to contact Christians; I just did not have the time. Once there was a ladies' prayer meeting in Taipei. Most of those ladies were wives of the high officials in the government. The leader of this group was the wife of the president. I was invited to speak to this group twice. In their prayer, they cried to the Lord sincerely. They confessed their sins, they asked for the Lord's mercy, and they prayed for the island of Taiwan. After their prayer, I spoke to them. Due to the fact that I was so busy, this was one of the few times that I went to speak to a group of Christians who did not meet with us. Even this, however, shows strongly that we did not cut ourselves off from other Christians, nor did we cut them off.

Some people may ask, "Why wouldn't you be one with them?" Actually, however, we are really one with them in Christ. Because of the divisions, organizations, and traditions, we have no way to be practically one with them. Also, because we have seen the vision of the type in the Old Testament concerning the remnant of God's people bearing God's testimony, we cannot go back to captivity in order to join our dear brothers who are still there in captivity. What we can do and what we expect is that many of the Lord's children will take His Word, leave their captivity, and come back to join us. Then we will rejoice with them. This is our standing, this is our situation, and this is our attitude.

We do not deny that there are thousands and thousands of genuine believers scattered among all the denominations; we love them and we would like to share all the truths we have received from the Lord with them, if they would be open. While I was traveling in northern China in 1937, all the denominations were open to me. The China Inland Mission churches were especially open. I had my first study of the book of Hebrews with them based upon Andrew Murray's book *The Holy of Holies*. I was also welcome among the Presbyterians, the Southern Baptists, and the Episcopalians. They were all open to me. Even today I am occupied greatly with the ministry for the churches. However, if the denominations would open to me, I would spare some time to go and share with them the truths the Lord has revealed to us. We are not sectarian nor narrow-minded, but regretfully, they would not open to us.

We surely recognize that all the genuine believers are our brothers and sisters in the Lord. Also, we fully admit that we are not the only members of the Body of Christ. We are just a small part, just as the returned captives in the Old Testament were just a small remnant of all of the chosen people of God. In addition, we are open to all the dear Christians. If time allowed and if they were open to us, I would take the lead to go and share the truth with them. We do love all the Lord's children and like to share with them all the truths that we have received of the Lord and that we have experienced and enjoyed.

Some may ask, "Why don't you invite others to come to your meetings to speak?" We did this in the past. One particular brother shared my training for a number of weeks. I asked him to speak every day. This shows that we are open to others. Also, on the island of Taiwan I wrote a letter of invitation to T. Austin-Sparks in London and he came to visit us twice. We stopped inviting him, however, because in his second visit he tried to tear down the ground of our work, which is the unique ground of the oneness of the church practice.

Our attitude is that we are open to all the saints. We do not consider that we only are the members of the Body of Christ. The most we consider is that we are members of the Body of Christ who have come back to the original, unique ground of oneness and who are standing here as God's remnant. The difference between other Christians and us is that they still remain there in their captivity, while we have come back to the proper, unique ground of oneness. We are open to all the believers, but we would not take the place of captivity where they remain. We could not join them in that place because it is a place of captivity, full of divisions, organizations, and traditions.

### PREACHING THE GOSPEL, TEACHING THE TRUTH, AND MINISTERING LIFE

During these last twenty years, the Lord has established His recovery in the United States. The Lord has been continually speaking to us, especially by opening up the New Testament to us, book after book. We must bear the responsibility to spread all these treasures that the Lord has shown us from His holy Word. We need to spread these treasures by preaching the gospel to the unsaved, teaching the truths to the saved ones, and ministering life to the seeking ones. All the saints who have returned to the proper and unique ground of oneness must bear this responsibility. This is why

we must train all the saints with the precious truths which
we have received from the Lord that each one may be qualified and enabled to spread these truths by preaching the
gospel, teaching the truth, and ministering life to people. We
not only love the Christians outside of us, but we also love all
human beings. The Lord loves the world and we need to be
the same. We love the world by preaching the gospel to them
and we love our fellow-Christians, even though they are not
with us, by teaching the truth and by ministering life to
them.

We all need to have a clear view concerning the Lord's
practice in His recovery. Then we can have a proper attitude.
We should never be sectarian, and we should always be open
to all people. We should not only be open to all the Christians,
but also be open to all the unbelievers. Because we have
received the Lord's mercy and we are now a people bearing
God's testimony in His truth and in His life, we must learn to
be open at all times to every Christian, teaching the truth
and ministering the life supply to them. When you meet other
Christians, do not be bothered that they are Christians in the
divisions. Do not change your attitude, but still be open to
them. Present the truth and minister life to them. Try not
to consider, think, or feel that they are different from the
saints who are with us because they also are our fellow-
believers in Christ.

Finally, we should never try to proselyte Christians from
the divisions. We must always do our best, on the other hand,
to preach the gospel, teach the truth, and minister life. Let
other Christians have their own choice regarding the matter
of the church. The Lord's testimony does not depend upon a
big number but upon the reality of His life. Even though we
may have a small number, if we live the reality of the life of
Christ, this is the testimony of Jesus. Even if we had twenty
million saints among us, without the reality of the life of
Christ, there would be no testimony; this does not mean
anything. This is why I feel that we should not pay that much
attention to the numerical increase. I believe that if we really
live a life of Christ as our reality, the increase will come. We

should live such a testimony. Then all the churches over the whole earth will bear the same testimony and will carry the same New Testament ministry to establish the same New Testament church as the Body of Christ. Then wherever people go, they will see the same thing. They will see different peoples, different races, different ranks, and different societies, meeting together, bearing the same testimony, and always speaking the same thing. They will see people speaking the same thing in many different languages and bearing the genuine testimony of Jesus. Even though we may have a small number, this is still something prevailing in the eyes of God.

I hope this fellowship helps us to have a proper spirit and to hold a right attitude toward all our fellow-believers. We must learn to love them and even to love every man. Our practice should be that we love our neighbors, our schoolmates, our colleagues, and all our friends.

When other Christians ask us where we fellowship, we should not pretend to be someone else. We should be frank and tell them what we are. Whether they would continue to be open to us or whether they would be closed to us is up to them. Regardless of their reaction, we still would love them and not argue with them. We must bear our responsibility. We must learn how to preach the gospel, present the truth, or minister life to them. If we would do these three things, the ones around us will receive something. We do not need to defend ourselves against negative speaking. It is better from the very beginning to let people know that you are meeting in a local church which is very much helped by the ministry of Witness Lee. If they would respond to you with something negative, do not argue with them. You need to present them a clear view of a biblical truth which the Lord has shown us. Maybe you would share John 3:14 with them. You might tell them that the Lord Jesus applied the type of the brass serpent to Himself, showing that when He was in the flesh, He was in "the likeness of the flesh of sin" (Rom. 8:3), which likeness was the form of the brass serpent. Tell them that when Christ, our Redeemer, was on the cross, He was lifted up like the brass serpent in the wilderness. Your presentation of this biblical truth will shock them. If you presented the truth in this way to your colleague every day, he would be subdued and enlightened. Eventually, he would be fully opened to the ministry you receive because he would realize that the truth is there.

This is one of the main factors why I called this urgent training. The ones who bear the responsibility of the churches must realize that we have to change our way in order to bring the saints fully into the truths of God's New Testament economy. If we train the saints, they will be enabled to preach the gospel, teach the truth, and minister life. We do not need to remain in our old practice where people meet with us for a number of years and still they have not been perfected to minister to others. They may appreciate the meetings and the ministry, but they still are not able to present the truth. May the Lord bring all the saints in all the churches fully into the truth, and may all the saints in the Lord's recovery be those who are enabled and skilled to preach the gospel, teach the truth, and minister life for the carrying out of God's New Testament economy unto the building up of the Body of Christ.